*The Year I Died*

www.pammenteryoung.com

ISBN-10: 1482714930
ISBN-13: 978-1482714937

Cover Design & Photography © Gadbois Photography
Author photograph © Gadbois Photography

CreateSpace Independent Publishing Platform
Printed in the United States of America

# THE YEAR I DIED

## A Memoir

### By

### Michelle Pammenter Young

Dear Gloria!

Thank you for your support.

Enjoy the book.

Michelle

*The Year I Died*

*This book is dedicated to my husband Wade who was my rock without whom I would not have come through to the other side of this horrific journey.*

*To my children Ben and Kate who continue to be my reasons to live.*

*Also to my beloved sister and her husband, your support during the tough days of late summer was invaluable.*

*Thanks to my dear friends Michele, Phil, Debbie, Chantal, Arlene, Rick, Lisa, Jenn P, Dale, Jenn L, Wendy and Amy.*

*Also to the many people who provided support in ways too numerous to mention.*

*Finally to my father James for raising me to be such a tough cookie and teaching me to never give up.*

*I love and cherish you all.*

*Thank You.*

*The Year I Died*

*With love to Chris and Tiny.*
*We had such a brief time together*
*and not a day goes by when you are not in my thoughts.*
*I miss you both with all my heart.*
*Until we meet again.*
*M*

The story you are about to read is based on actual events. Names have been changed in order to protect the privacy of certain individuals.

Life should NOT be a journey to the grave with the intention of arriving safely in an attractive and well preserved body, but rather to skid in sideways - Champagne in one hand - chocolate in the other - body thoroughly used up, totally worn out and screaming 'WOO HOO, What a Ride.
--Unknown

# PROLOGUE

I flip my legs over the side of the bed and rush the twelve or so feet to the ensuite bathroom, throw myself on my knees and just manage to grab the toilet bowl before the surge starts. Over and over again I retch, at first there is a little bit to come up. I haven't been eating much lately, so I'm surprised there is anything. Then for the next ten minutes I yoyo between lying on the floor exhausted, to hanging onto the toilet retching, my body wracked by dry heaves.

Finally the nausea subsides and I quietly curl up into a ball on the carpeted bathroom floor breathing shallowly. "I can't take this anymore," I think as the slow sound of a deep howl begins to escape my throat. The feeling of nausea is replaced with something far worse: a deep sense of pain, of loss, of regret and of horror. How can this be happening to me? Surely this is some horrific nightmare from which I will soon awaken and give a sigh of relief that it's over. I hold onto my knees and sob and sob, feeling my chest heave and the palms of my hands ache. I'm not sure why, but my palms always ache when I'm experiencing heartbreak, although this is not heartbreak, this is something beyond heartbreak.

I cry out of sadness, out of frustration, how, how can this be happening to me? I have a great life. It's always been good. I mean, I've had my ups and downs, but really when I look around me at what I've been able to achieve and how I live, I consider myself pretty lucky. Perhaps, some would say I've worked for it, and yes perhaps I have, I am a driver after all - Miss Type A personality - always wanting to be at the top. Is that why this is happening to me? Was life too good? Did I do something to make this happen to me? I lie here on the floor questioning myself, questioning my life, breaking it down into chapters and moments to try and find the fatal flaw. The thing I did to make it all go so wrong, or perhaps the things I have done that contributed to this.

I think back to my early childhood, I was born in South Africa in the sixties when it was still relatively safe there. I had a great childhood. I was adopted at a very young age and my parents always loved me. They may have been incredibly strict and sometimes over the top with their rules, but they raised me well and showed me the value of working hard as well as enjoying life. When I was quite young we lived in Kloof in what was then the Natal Province of South Africa. It was an incredible place to live; I will always remember the warm winds that used to circle our house. My father had built a beautiful house for us; it was round, like a doughnut. We loved that house my brother, sister and I. Yes, I had a brother, who was adopted when I was one and a sister, also adopted when I was almost four. We did have another baby brother, Bussy was his name, he was only a foster child and unfortunately his family took him back after four years. That was the first time I recall my mother having her heart broken. I don't think she ever recovered from that and in some ways that event tore the family apart, ever so slightly. Not enough that you would notice, but enough that there was a tiny fissure which would eventually grow over the years until it cracked, but that is another story.

My brother Sean and my sister Marie and I were typical kids; we loved playing outside, loved getting into trouble, and of course fought like all normal siblings do. We were very lucky in that we travelled to Germany a lot as children to spend Christmas with our cousins, as well as fortunate enough to spend many trips with our family in and around South Africa. Our education was both worldly and practical. My mother Jackie stayed home with us and although she was a typical mother of the sixties when children should be seen and not heard, she also spent some wonderful times with us. I recall sitting on her lap in the evening as she read us our bedtime stories. After the story I'd ask, "Mummy, tell me the story about how you adopted me", and she'd smile and hug me tighter and tell me the lovely story. The story about how she wanted children so very badly, but couldn't have any of her own, and then she got a call that there was a little baby girl in Durban and would she like to come and meet her. Mummy said that the minute she laid eyes on me she loved me and wanted me and so I always felt chosen and blessed.

So why, if I was chosen and blessed and loved did I end up here, curled up in a ball on my bathroom floor begging for a different life. Oh well I think, as I pick myself back up. I must go on. I cannot quit. I must continue to work through this, if not for myself, then for my children and my husband and my family, my dear mother and father and my younger brother and sister who love me.

I check the time on my iPhone before I climb back into bed. It is three in the morning, Vancouver time, and another sleepless night I think, as I lie down exhausted from sickness and the emotional breakdown I have just had. At least it is officially the shortest night of the year. I close my eyes and feel myself gently drifting off into sleep; I relish this, a place where for a short time I can forget. My last thought before I slip into dreamland is "I guess it can't get any worse than this". Boy was I wrong.

## HAPPY NEW YEAR

"Mum, mum, wake up. Mum it's almost midnight, wake up." "Mmmm" I mumble as I slowly open my eyes and see my daughter Rose looking at me intently. "We need to watch the countdown clock in New York City Mum, and then can we go outside and bang pots and pans?" she asks. Oh yes, I remember, it's New Year's Eve and I promised her I would stay up until midnight. Rose is ten and already she is able to stay up later than I am, but then again, I've never been a night owl.

"All right", I say, "have you been awake the whole time?"

"Yes Mum, I've been watching all the celebrations on TV, I can't believe it's going to be 2012 soon." Rose says excitedly. She gets off the couch and runs to get pots and pans while I sit up trying to feel more awake. It's just Rose and I this year for New Years Eve. My wonderful husband Bob is away working in Australia and my son Kory is spending the evening with friends. I guess since it's the start of a new year, I should introduce myself.

My name is Michelle; I'm a young forty-six year old mother of two with a zest for life. I work as a Financial Advisor for a major insurance company and spend most of my days working from home or my office on the Sunshine Coast. My family and I live in a lovely house in a quiet neighbourhood with our sweet dog Waldo and our crazy attack cat Bella.

I came to Canada in 1979 after fourteen formative years in South Africa. I was not happy about being uprooted and moved to another country and I hated the cold weather. Also, just before moving to Canada I had seen the movie Earthquake and I remember hearing that Vancouver was between the San Andreas and Juan de Fuca fault, so I was terrified that we were moving to a new land fraught with earthquakes and volcanoes. As it turned out, I really had nothing to worry about. We haven't had any significant earthquakes or active volcanoes, although the eruption of Mount Saint Helens only a few months after our arrival, on my brother's birthday, was rather auspicious.

I spent most of my teens and young twenties living in the Vancouver area and travelling when I could. My passion for travel began as child and is still with me today. Much to my father's dismay, I spend far too much money on travel and far too little on saving for retirement.

I met my first husband in my late twenties; we married, moved to Squamish and had two children. I started my first business, BundleBag, at the age of thirty-four. Running a business was a huge learning experience for me. For a woman who rarely balanced her cheque book, I now had to learn how to read a balance sheet, predict trends, keep ahead of the competition, create innovative products and all the while be profitable. There were days it worked and days it didn't. Two years into the business my marriage dissolved and I found myself renting a townhouse and sharing custody of the children with their father.  For five years I was single again.  These years were full of ups and downs.  I loved being on my own, managing my own time, working until all hours of the morning if I needed to and taking a break for a run when my body screamed stress.

Kory and Rose were the center of my world and they were lovely human beings.  Kory was such a serious little boy; he was an avid reader and would spend many hours engrossed in a book or doing jigsaw puzzles.  Rose on the other hand was a free spirit, wild child, not unlike her mother.  She loved water and could often be counted on to strip down to her birthday suit and dip into even the smallest of puddles.  My heart would swell with love when the two of them were sitting on my lap reading.  "Mummy," Kory would say, "again, read it again please Mummy", so I'd turn back the pages and start the book from the beginning.  At bedtime, their little eyes would look at me with a mixture of love and a glint of manipulation as they asked, "can we cuddle with you in your bed please Mummy?"  Who could turn that request down, they had me at the "please Mummy" and they knew it.  I loved cuddling with them, although, even though they were little, a king sized bed was not big enough for three people.

In 2007 I met my husband Bob.  I'm embarrassed to say we met at a bar, and not just any bar, but in my opinion, the worst bar in town.  I know you're thinking, "Why would I be in the worst bar in town?"  Well, in a small town, there aren't many options after ten at night, and so one evening I found myself hanging with friends at a local watering hole enjoying a cold Heineken. I looked across the room and a handsome man caught my eye. He had the bluest eyes I had ever seen and he was looking at me with this huge grin that never left his face. Five years later, we are now married, have added Waldo, our dog, to the family, and my husband is still wowing me with his beautiful eyes and his huge happy grin.

Bob is a helicopter pilot. He was born in Canada and has one daughter Anna, now an adult and an amazingly talented singer. Anna is away studying to become a teacher and Bob is currently on a contract in Australia, which is why he is not here to celebrate New Years Eve with us. I miss him, and wish we could have been together, but I will see him soon. In only six weeks I will be heading to Australia to spend two weeks with him. In the meantime, Rose is keeping me company and doing a very good job of getting me into the New Year's spirit judging from all the clanging I can hear coming from the kitchen.

She bounds back into the living room, pots in hand as the final countdown begins on the television. Ten, nine, eight, seven, six, five, four, three, two, one…Happy New Year! Rose jumps up and down screaming "Happy New Year"; she runs to the door and begins clanging pots and pans. I can hear the entire neighbourhood cheering as I come to the door and bang my own pots. "It's 2012 Mum", Rose exclaims as she drops everything to give me a great big hug. "Yes honey, and it's going to be a fantastic year, we're going to have so much fun," I say with a laugh, "now let's get back inside, put these pots and pans away and go to bed". After much cajoling I finally have Rose curled up next to me in bed and the two of us drift off into dreamland.

The next day Kory joins us and we spend a quiet day at home getting ready for back to school. The kids start back in a few days, however, I'm back at work tomorrow and January is going to be a busy month. Not only do I have a lot of client appointments lined up, but I'm also studying for my Mutual Fund License. I hate studying. At my age it's like pouring water into a sieve and expecting it to fill up, nothing stays. I sit down with the greatest of intentions, and then within thirty minutes I've fallen asleep over my book and will have to start all over again. At this rate I'll never absorb the material. I'm also waiting to hear if I have achieved 'Convention Level' with work. 2011 was my first full year in my new career and my goal was to build a happy client base and achieve gold status. I am pretty certain I have it, but will find out for sure in the next week or so.

The days pass quickly now. Kory and Rose are back in school and I'm back at work full swing. It is nine-forty five in the morning and I'm sitting in my car on the ferry. Today I am working from my Gibson's office and have a full day of client meetings booked. I open my laptop to review my notes for the day and check a few emails. As my email loads I grab my travel blanket and cover my legs. It's freezing in the car. I hate winter, having been raised in South Africa, I love the heat and although I've lived in Canada for over thirty years now, I will never get used to the cold. I could go upstairs and sit on the heated passenger deck of the ferry, but then I'd be wasting valuable work time going up there, finding a spot, getting all set up etc. Here I keep my laptop on my passenger seat and I'm good to go.

Fifty-seven new messages bound into my inbox. I quickly scan them to find those relevant for today or any urgent emails that need actioning before my busy day. Immediately an email grabs my attention. "Congratulations", it says, "You have achieved Convention Level".

"Yippee", I squeal out loud in my car. Now Bob and I will get to go to San Antonio, Texas, in March, and the trip luckily coincides with my birthday. This news just makes my day. I wish it were not four-forty five in the wee hours of the morning in Australia; I'd love to call Bob and give him the news. I'll just have to settle for an email. I forward the email on to Bob and finish responding to emails just as the ferry begins to dock.

My appointments take me right through until six o'clock. I'm tired and hungry, I think, as I drive to my mother's house. Mum lives in Sechelt with her husband Basil, and I stay with her when I'm working over here. Basil is a grumpy old sod, so mum really enjoys it when I visit. Most of the time we go out for dinner, or eat something simple at her place, then spend the evening watching HGTV. Mum and I have had our ups and downs over the years, but lately we have become close, particularly since I started working on the Coast. Tonight we are staying in as the weather is bad and mum didn't feel like braving the cold. My last appointment was in Sechelt, so it was only a two-minute drive to mum's. "Good thing," I think. Missing lunch was a very bad plan.

After a delicious meal of sausages, mashed potatoes and peas – my favourite – we settle into her room with cups of tea. I'm excited for my trip to Australia in a few weeks so we chat about that and about travel in general.

Mum spends a few months every summer with her sister Stephanie in Germany; it is her relaxing time, and something she looks forward to every year.

"Mum", I ask, "when are you going to see Auntie Stephanie this year?"

"I don't know", she sighs, "I have to wait to see how Basil is doing, his leg has been bothering him a lot and I don't want to leave him until that gets a little better." At eighty-nine, Basil has a few health issues. Mentally he's still with it, but his body is starting to break down after so many years on this earth and although he doesn't claim to need any help getting around, mum is still worried about leaving him unless he is fully well.

"Will Gladys look after him again when you are gone?" I ask.

"Yes, she will come in three times a week to prepare his meals, do his laundry and make sure everything is alright, she is a Godsend", mum intones.

Gladys has been working for mum and Basil for many years now and is the only person who can tolerate his moods. I have never figured out why mum married Basil; he is a racist, arrogant, chauvinist. He controls mum with his moods and is so rude that most of their friends refuse to visit anymore. My mother has had a very hard life. Without getting into any details, suffice it to say, she was neglected and abused by her mother most of her life. At twenty, mum fell in love with a wonderful man, he loved her and asked her to marry him, however, her mother said she was too young and would not allow the marriage to happen and she barred my mother from ever seeing him again. Unbeknownst to my grandmother, the two of them kept in contact over the years, but the physical separation proved too much for this man and he eventually sought the arms of another woman. As temporary as this was, it was a breaking point for my mother, who believed in fully honouring their engagement and was devastated by the dalliance. She refused further contact and a few years later, met another man. Unfortunately for her, he was as controlling and abusive as her mother, more so if the truth be told. They married in a hasty fashion without the blessing of the family and so began my mother's few years of hell. This first husband treated her in such a way that she not only felt powerless, she came to believe she was completely worthless. I don't think my mother ever overcame the damage done to her by both her mother and this man, even after she divorced him. My mother met and married my father a few years later and to all intents and purposes theirs was a normal marriage that ended a few years after we arrived in Canada. How mum came to ever marry a man like Basil, I will never know, but looking a little bit at her past, particularly her mother's influence and that of her first husband, helps me to understand a little bit why she felt she needed him. You see, mum, as a result of her early life experiences never felt confident enough to make her own decisions, and when a bossy, arrogant man like Basil came along, to mum she saw a strong, supporting partner.

What she didn't know is that over the years his personality and controlling behavior would isolate both her family and her friends. Until I started staying overnight with mum, I had no idea how much he had lied to my brother, sister and I, and in doing so, he kept us away from our mother. Now, that I am here, I see things that break my heart. I see the way he treats mum and I am angry. I would never say anything as it might make mum's life more miserable but I certainly won't cater to him. His arrogance towards me when I walk in the door is unbelievable. His condescending and sometimes sexually offensive remarks make me sick. No wonder mum likes to go away to be with her sister as often as she can.

I watch with a mixture of sadness and anger as mum sits outside to have a cigarette. I can feel her thoughts; she is biding her time until she can get to see her sister again. This is not where she wants to be. She stays out of obligation, but given a choice, she would move to Germany in an instant and do her holidays here to visit her grandchildren and us. How sad she must feel, how lonely. I feel a pang of regret that I haven't spent more time visiting her over the years. I can make a hundred different excuses, kids, work, etc., but they would simply be excuses. The truth of the matter is that I could come here anytime, and should make more of an effort to do so, especially with the children.

Mum comes back inside and we settle down to watch "Love it or List it", one of our favourite shows. We giggle and ooh and aah like two little girls, watching back-to-back shows until it's time for us to go to bed.

"Don't forget to wake me up at six so I can take my medicine," mum says.

"I won't forget mum, I'll tickle your feet like I did last time okay?"

"Yes," she laughs, "that would be nice."

# WAITING

Wow, time is flying. I have only ten more days before I leave to see Bob in Australia and I'm so excited I'm bouncing off the walls. I've been packed for almost three weeks now. Since I am going to a summer climate I packed everything except my underwear and cosmetics. I certainly won't be wearing shorts and a bathing suit here anytime soon. I have decided to use my iPhone to do a vlog (video blog) of my trip to keep everyone up to date, so will be bringing both my new iPhone 4 and my old iPhone 3S for use in the more remote locations. This way if the old phone gets stolen or dropped in the ocean I won't be too concerned about it.

I have a little countdown app on my iPhone and literally bubble over with excitement each time I look at it and watch the hours tick by. Work right now is crazy busy. I got the good news that I had passed my Mutual Fund exam and since then clients have been calling me to move their funds, open RRSP's and discuss education funds for their children. I had no idea how much things would take off once I got licensed and I am grateful that my clients trust me enough to want to move more of their business over to me. Although the insurance side really is my passion, I am enjoying the conversations that working on the wealth side brings forward. As I sit here reading at the end of a long day I realize how grateful I am. Not only do I love what I do, I am also able to make a living at it and contribute to my family. I truly think I am blessed, I have a terrific career and I get the time to travel with my husband.

A great yawn escapes me and I realize if I don't get to bed soon I'll be a write off tomorrow. I have two complicated meetings set up for tomorrow and need my wits about me. "Waldo," I call. "Waldo, where are you?" He comes bounding up the stairs and hops on the bed. For a puggle, Waldo is pretty big, but he still loves to cuddle and with Bob away I rely on Waldo to keep me safe. Not that he is the best guard dog, if a stranger came to the door he would simply roll over and beg him to rub his tummy, and he never barks. Fat lot of good he does in the security department. He is however a master in the loving department, he's always happy to see me and unlike the children, he never talks back. "There's a good boy," I say as he curls up beside me. I reach over, turn out the light and soon I am asleep dreaming of cruising in the South Pacific.

It is all black and I cannot see anything. "Hello, hello can anyone hear me?" "Mum, dad are you there?" I ask, the panic just beginning to register in my voice. I see a shadow run past my window and then hear my fathers' voice.

"I'm in here Michelle". I go running down the dark hallway but cannot find him.

"Dad", I scream, "dad where are you?" There is no answer, I can feel someone near me, know they are watching me. Whoever or whatever it is, I know it is pure evil. Like some black monster I can sense its presence around me. I try to find my dad again, where did he go? I slide my hands along the wall trying to find a light switch, where the heck is the switch? I am careful, I don't want to make too much noise, and I don't want this thing to get me. Then I see it, it's running towards me, eyes glowing like lit coal, its mouth curled in a viscous black teethed grimace. "I'm coming it says, I've got you."

"No", I scream, "daddy, daddy, daddy," I'm screaming at the top of my lungs as I run up the stairs. The creature is right behind me, I can feel its heat, and then suddenly its claw clips my ankle. I lurch forward and push with all my might and fly through the door, landing on the floor in my room, my mind pushing and pushing away from this evil as I slowly awake into consciousness. I am lying on my back in my bed, my heart racing, fear pumping through my body, my eyes wide in shock. Can this really be only a dream? It seems too real; my dog Waldo is alert as well, sitting looking at me. Surely that's not a good sign. Did he see it too? I am too scared and stunned to move, my eyes slowly take in the room around me - everything looks okay. It's too dark though, so I turn on the light, pull my quilt up to my chin and lie there waiting for my adrenaline level to drop and my fear to subside. So much for getting a good nights sleep.

# AUSTRALIA

Today is the day. I am so excited; I've been packed for almost a month and have been counting down the days. Now it is only a few hours before my flight leaves for Sydney. I've said goodbye to my kids, lots of hugs and promises to bring back something cool for them.

As I pull out of my driveway I run through my mental checklist. "Passport, check! Tickets, check! Visa Card, check! Ipad, check! Headset, check! Book, Check!" I'm good to go.

It is a nice, albeit crisp early evening in Sea to Sky country and the drive to Vancouver is beautiful. I am meeting Debbie for bubbly before heading over to my dad's. My flight isn't leaving until almost midnight this evening so I have lots of time to relax.

The Cactus Club is busy as usual but I easily spot Debbie at the bar. "Hey Honey, how are you?" I ask, giving her a big hug.

"Good," she says making room for me next to her, "you must be so excited. I've ordered us a bottle of bubbly, how are you getting to the airport?"

"My sister is taking me," I say. "My dad says I can leave my car in his garage, so that will save on airport parking. How is work?"

"The usual crap, this industry never changes." Debbie remarks. She and I were one of the first couple of women to sell in the computer industry way back in the day. It has been over twenty-five years and Debbie is still there. She's very good at what she does, the money is decent and the clients enjoy her, so why change something that is working.

Our bubbly arrives and we make a toast to a great holiday down under. After some good conversation, and a few friendly comments from the local guys, Debbie and I head out. She walks to her apartment a few blocks away and I drive over to dad's.

My dad Ben and his wife Tina live in an amazing condo overlooking downtown Vancouver. Tina is a vivacious lady who has made my father very happy. They are both now retired, although my father, being the workaholic that he always was, contracts his services out about half the time.

Like most little girls, my father has always been the center of my world. When I was growing up, I used to think he could do nothing wrong. Now that I am all grown up, I realize he has flaws just like everyone else but I still look up to him tremendously. It is from my father that I get my work ethic, my punctuality and my drive. I suspect a lot of my drive to achieve and succeed is in some way to please my father - regardless it serves me well.

"It would be wonderful to do another family holiday like our river rafting trip in the early 90s," I think, as I pull up to my father's garage. I'll never forget that short weekend holiday that my brother, sister, father and I took, a two-day river-rafting trip down the Thompson River. It was so much fun crashing down the river together in the raft, getting freezing cold, soaking wet and laughing and laughing until our cheeks hurt. We camped on a little island in the middle of the river. The campsite was extremely rustic. The toilet was a broken shack in the middle of the woods completely exposed except that the side facing the campsite was a wooden wall. One could sit on the loo and watch the trains go by. I have some terrific memories from that weekend, one of the funniest was in the morning when my father opened a beer for breakfast and he said to me, "When there isn't water, one can always a drink beer no matter what the time of day."

Shortly after parking my car at dad's my sister Marie and her husband Jeff picked me up. We are going to dinner at a new Japanese restaurant on Cambie Street. There was a huge line out the door when we arrived and we weren't sure if we would manage to get a table in time. However, as luck would have it, a few seats became available at the counter. The meal was very good, and in no time we were back in her car on our way to the airport.

In typical Michelle fashion, I was four hours early for my flight. The attendant told me the flight was fully booked so seating choice was limited, but thankfully I managed to get an aisle seat. Once through customs I found my way to a little spot where I could have a glass of wine and wait for my flight. I made a few phone calls to mum, the kids and a couple of friends to say goodbye before it got too late, then spent the rest of the time surfing the web. By ten o'clock I was starting to fade, my normal bedtime is between nine and ten so I was struggling to stay up for boarding at eleven. I took a quick look at the board showing flight details only to notice that unfortunately my flight was over an hour delayed. "Damn," I thought, "how the heck can I stay up this late?" Well, nothing else to do but to have another glass of wine. Finally at around one-fifteen in the morning the plane was fully boarded and we were ready to leave. I took one of mum's lovely little sleeping tablets, closed my eyes and drifted off.

Sixteen hours later I arrived in Sydney. I was so excited to see my husband I couldn't get off that plane fast enough. Fortunately going through customs was very quick and soon I was running down the ramp and into his arms. We were like a couple of teenagers, we couldn't take our hands off each other and were bubbling over with excitement, our words falling all over each other as we rushed to speak. We took the train to King's Cross where we had rented a lovely hotel room in Springfield Lodge. The hotel itself was quite nice but the room was a bit of a shock; I don't think it was larger than ten feet square. It didn't matter, we were only here for a couple of nights and there was certainly enough room for me to do my workouts in a little spot in the corner.

After dropping off the luggage and a brief freshen up, we took the train down to Bondi Beach. It was lovely, but I was so excited to see Bob that it could have been a snowstorm and I would still have enjoyed it. We found a decent restaurant overlooking Bondi Beach, sat at a window seat and spent a few hours chatting and catching up.  In two days it was Valentine's Day and we were getting on a ten-day cruise to the South Pacific.  The following day was the fifth anniversary of the day we met so we had lots to celebrate.

"Are you happy love?" Bob asked.

"I'm ecstatic honey.  I'm so excited to see you and I can't wait to get on the cruise.  I'm also excited to be going scuba diving again." I chimed.

"Me too," he said "I can't believe it's been over six weeks since we last saw each other."

"I know," I said, holding his hand "the last week was the hardest, I think because I knew I would see you soon."

We sat there grinning like two cats that had eaten a couple of canaries.  Holding hands, gazing into each other's eyes completely oblivious to the world around us.  "This is love," I thought, "look at us happy as clams without a care in the world."

After a few hours we took the train back to our hotel and rested.  I was jetlagged from having flown over 16 hours across the world's largest ocean and Bob was tired from having spent the night up anxious to see me.

We spent that evening wandering around the King's Cross area looking for a place to eat, found a terrific pizza joint, enjoyed a lovely meal with wine and local beer and then walked around like tourists enjoying the night-time sights and sounds of King's Cross in the evening.

I woke the next morning bright and early, refreshed and ready to spend the day on Manly Beach.  Bob went across the street to get a couple of coffees while I did my workout in a tiny little corner of the room. Once complete I shimmied myself into the tiny shower in the tiny bathroom, got cleaned up, put on my hot little bikini under my shorts and top and got ready to head out to the beach. Bob arrived back and, with coffee in hand; we went down to the train station.

The trip to Manly Beach was beautiful. We took a train down to the wharf and then boarded a ferry for a fifteen-minute ride across to the other side of the harbour. The view from the ferry was spectacular. We could see all of Sydney Harbour, the bridge, the Sydney Opera House, and the beautiful architecture all the while basking in the warm Australian summer heat. Once the ferry docked we swarmed along with the masses for about two blocks until we reached Manly Beach. The beach itself was stunning, a long stretch of sand, blue ocean with waves and hardly any people on the shore. Although it was a lovely sunny day, Australia had experienced a rather wet summer up until this point so the water was too cold for me to swim in. I did however have a quick dip and then lay back on the beach sand, drying off and warming like a beached whale. Okay, perhaps whale wouldn't be the best comparison.

After a little while we walked down the beach, watched a little bit of a surfing championship contest and chose a spot to have lunch. One of the things I love about being in a hot climate is that no matter what time of day it is, it always feels like beer time. In that hot Australian heat a nice chilled Fosters lager goes down in no time.

Soon it was time to take the ferry back across the water to our hotel in King's Cross. We showered off the beach sand and Bob poured us a couple of Caesars, from the Clamato juice that I had brought with me. It was so nice to be together again, so relaxing, so perfect. We chatted for a couple of hours and then headed out for dinner. Tomorrow was going to be a big day and an early morning. We had to be up at the crack of dawn to pack our bags and take the train down to the station by the pier so we could board the ship at our predetermined time.

The next day I was literally jumping out of my shoes with excitement and could not contain myself. Normally not an early riser, I was awake an hour prior to the alarm going off, lying there, eyes wide open, waiting to pack my bags, take the train and get on our ship. We got to the pier in time, checked our luggage in and walked to a local coffee shop to have a nice cappuccino or, as the Australians call it, a long flat white.

An hour later we were walking up the gangway onto the ship. It didn't take long to find our cabin, which although small was lovely and clean. We normally try to get a balcony cabin but this being a ten-day cruise and relatively expensive, considering I'd flown halfway around the world, we decided to settle for an oceanview cabin. Later on in the cruise I realized this was the right choice, as one evening I walked down the hallway and passed a woman whose cabin door was open as well as her balcony door. The heat wafting through her cabin into the hallway was almost unbearable for me. Having a balcony would not have proved to be a plus on that cruise. As is typical with most cruises there was a Sail Away Party on the top deck. P&O Cruises really did a great job with this. The music was fantastic, the drinks were flowing, the people were laughing and of course the sun was shining. It was absolutely wonderful as we made our slow exit out from Sydney Harbour, watching all the beautiful sights of the city pass us by. It took almost an hour to get out to the ocean and during this time the music continued to play, the drinks continued to flow and people continued to laugh joyously as they got to know one another. I knew this was going to be an incredible cruise and both Bob and I would enjoy every single day not just for the fact that we were together for the first time in six weeks but also because we were going to be spending time in a tropical place with what seemed like a great fun group of people.

After leaving Sydney, we sailed overnight and followed that up with one full day at sea. Bob and I spent this day exploring the ship and finding out everything it had to offer. There were some great places like the Oasis at the back of the ship, which proved to be one of my favourite spots throughout the entire cruise. This was my tenth cruise and Bobs sixth cruise, so we have certain expectations when it comes to the ship and the experience on a cruise holiday. We tend to choose cruises that have more stops in port, than those where you are just floating in the sea. This allows us to do something different almost every day and to see new places that we may not have seen if it weren't for the cruise.

Our first stop was Port Vila on the island of Vanuatu. Bob and I walked off the ship and found a local taxi to take us into town to the spot where I had pre-booked Scuba Diving. We were supposed to dive the Cathedral dive, but a storm was to come in which would make the dive impossible, so we had to choose a different location. We were very fortunate in that it was only a small group so Bob and I ended up with our own guide throughout the diving experience. I have a mild form of exercise-induced asthma and scuba diving can be a little precarious for me. We always make sure to tell our dive buddy this once on board the boat on the way to the site otherwise they may possibly not let me dive. As it turned out I did have an asthma issue on this particular dive but our dive buddy was very good. As soon as I notified him that I was having breathing difficulties we ascended to around the fifteen foot mark and he checked to make sure I was okay, we swam at this level for a bit and then began a descent back down. It was a spectacular dive and we saw many brightly coloured fish of all shapes and sizes. We saw sea urchins, sea cucumbers, puffer fish and so many others, the names of which I couldn't remember even if you'd told me a hundred times.

A few hours later we were sitting in the Numbawan Cafe enjoying a cold beer with our fellow divers. As it turned out, one of the divers was the chief engineer on the ship so of course we had to ask him what it was like to work on an older ship.

"It's very frustrating," he said "everything keeps breaking down and we are continually having to repair and replace things.  Fortunately I'm almost at the end of my three-month stint on this ship and will be able to go on a much newer ship next time."

"I have noticed the noises from the ships engine much louder than any in my past experience," I told him "and especially the sound from the ships stabilizers." "Every time they get extended it sounds like the ship is being torn apart."

He laughed, "Don't worry she is a seaworthy ship however she is certainly long in the tooth."

"Thank goodness for that," I thought.  "The last thing I need is for this ship to sink and I die ten or twenty thousand miles from home."

That night we got back to the ship rather late.  I think we were one of the last few on board before she lifted the gangways.  We had dinner in the dining room and although the food was okay I wasn't impressed with the fact that I had to put up a battle requesting that Bob and I get a table for two rather than sharing a table.  I tried to make it clear to them that throughout the cruise we would be requesting a table for two and if we could have this specific table, that would be great, I'm not sure if they really understood me.  I went to bed early as is my fashion and Bob stayed up little longer to enjoy the evening activities on the ship.

We spent the next day at an amazing resort on

Escapade Island.  This is one of those places you see in the high-end travel magazines with the individual thatched roof huts perched atop the sea.  The island was tiny and fortunately there was hardly anybody there so we felt as if we had the place to ourselves.  We leisurely snorkelled up and down the bay, lay in the sun to dry off and then jumped back in for another snorkel when we became too hot.

"Now this is the life." I said to Bob with a smile on my face. "Imagine if we could do this every day."

Bob laughed, "you'd love that, wouldn't you honey?"

"Yes, if only I could figure out a way to make a living remotely so that we can enjoy this any time we want.  You're so lucky with your career you could live anywhere and fly to work.  I really should try to find a way that I can do this, and once the children are old enough we can travel and live around the world and bring them with us every once in a while if they choose to, although they probably won't want to be with me when they're older.  Wouldn't that be fun honey?"

Bob reached over and took my hand.   "I'll do anything that makes you happy, love.  I'll live anywhere in the world.  I know you like warm places so if we can make this work let's do it."

I smile at him thinking, "My beautiful loving husband, I truly am lucky to have you."

After swimming we headed over to the restaurant on the resort for a nice light lunch, a glass of champagne for me and a nice beer for Bob.  We relaxed by the pool for the next hour or so until it was time for the ferry to take us back to our ship. Once on board I found myself a spot in the Oasis, ordered some bubbly and spent the rest of the afternoon lying there reading my book, enjoying the sunshine, and the cool breeze coming from the ocean, and sipping on sparkling bubbles.

Most of the rest of our ten days followed pretty much like that. We would get up early and get out onto some beautiful tropical island to spend the day snorkeling, swimming, walking along the beach and sampling the local food and cold beer.

My favourite stop was Champagne Bay, Vanuatu. This was one of the most spectacular beaches I had ever seen in my lifetime. We got off the ship early and found a local woman selling tours along the island. As there was no place to dive, the next best thing here was to snorkel so we chose to go to the Blue Hole, a spot where an underground river comes out and forms a small lake (hole) filled with fresh water and lots of beautiful fish. The freshwater at the far edge of the hole merges with the ocean water as the river comes out to the sea.

After a twenty-five minute taxi ride we finally arrive at a spot on the side of the road. There we see a few locals sitting under trees as well as a group of them huddled together at the top of what looks like a trail heading off into the jungle. Although he doesn't speak English, our driver assures us that this is the spot and that we are to follow those men where they take us. Feeling a little nervous about this we ask our driver to please stay so that he can take us back when we're finished. Bob turns to meet my eyes and I know without saying anything that we are both thinking the same thing. "Will this guy really stay here for us and be here in two hours?"

We walk up to the group of men huddled at the top of the trail and sure enough, one of them directs us to follow him down a windy and slightly tight jungle trail. For us it is no problem but I can see that this would challenge tourists who perhaps have difficulty walking. Five minutes later we are standing on the shore looking into a beautiful deep dark blue body of water. If you look and follow the way the water flows you can see a smaller dark blue hole or lake portion of water and then in the distance you can see and hear the sound of the waves from the ocean rushing in to meet this fresh water.

We quickly don our snorkels and masks, and jump into the water. It is bloody freezing. I was not expecting this. The man who walked us down here is looking at us with a little grin on his face. He is probably thinking, "silly tourists, what did you expect, this is an underground river." Nevertheless we acclimatize relatively quickly and begin exploring the area. Under water there are lots of old trees with gnarled branches where lots of lovely brightly coloured fish race around looking for food. I'm glad I brought my underwater camera for this excursion because I have never seen such tiny neon bright fish, and I'd like to have some photos to remind me of them.

Two hours later we climb the jungle trail back up to the top and sure enough there is our reliable driver sitting waiting for us. We make the return trip back along the bumpy, dusty road and after giving our driver a rather large tip we trot on foot to the ocean. This beach is so spectacular words cannot describe it. It has pure white sand similar to what you see in postcards of idyllic beach spots. It has those large tropical trees that are low to the ground with big branches extending out in all directions and big lush leaves on them. I have truly found my paradise. I would return to this beach in a heartbeat. After walking along the beach for a short while we enter one of the local vendors ramshackle food stands, pull up a couple of stools and order some ice-cold beer and peanuts. I sit there smiling from ear to ear; I don't think I've ever been happier than this. I leave Bob and go for a long swim in the ocean. It is warm, crystal clear, full of fish and just the right amount of salinity to make one comfortably buoyant. The only thoughts going through my head are - paradise, paradise, this is the life. I drift there without a care in the world, completely oblivious and without any knowledge of how drastically things will change for me over the next few months. Ignorance is bliss.

Champagne Bay is our last stop on this ten-day cruise and soon we are heading back to Sydney. For me back to Sydney means back home to Canada and away from Bob. For Bob, going back to Sydney means hopping on a flight to Papua New Guinea where he will spend the next six weeks working. Although we still have two days left at sea I am saddened. I do not want to say goodbye to

Bob and wish he were coming home with me. I know he will be back in Canada within a few weeks but right now it seems like an eternity.

We make the most of the last two days, spending precious time together. Once the ship docks back in Sydney we take the train to the hotel we stayed in just ten days ago. That evening we find a very unique outdoor restaurant to eat at, a few blocks from our hotel. We are both rather subdued and wish this wasn't our last supper. Thankfully the energy of the restaurant picks up our spirits and we have a wonderful last evening together.

At the airport the next day we hold onto each other tightly as we say our teary goodbyes. It is so hard to leave now, so hard to be apart after spending so much wonderful time together over the last twelve days. It takes great strength to tear ourselves away from each other, and we watch with tears in our eyes as each of us walks towards our separate gates.

## WARNING SIGNS

I had a hard time adjusting to my first few days back in Canada. I missed my husband tremendously and the weather was awful. I was used to warm summer sunshine and here I was trudging around in ice and snow, definitely not my cup of tea. The only blessing was to be able to be back with my kids, although I have to admit, that wore off after about the first week. I was insanely busy at work, which helped keep my mind off the fact that Bob was still going to be away for a few more weeks. I did however have something amazing to look forward to. At the end of March, I, along with some of my work colleagues, would be going to San Antonio, Texas for Convention. The best part was that Bob was going to be able to come home early on the twenty-third of March so he could go with me.

Eventually I got back into the flow of things. I spent a few days over on the Sunshine Coast meeting with clients and got to spend some great time with mum again. The busier I was the happier I was, so I made certain to pack my days with appointments from nine until six, rarely taking time for lunch. When I wasn't sitting down with clients face-to-face, I was planning the business for the year or acting as a taxi driver for my children. The time flew by and soon it was early March. The weather had started to improve and although there still weren't any blossoms on the trees, one had the hope that spring wasn't too far away. I was happy and things were organized, I'm always happy when things are organized, and life was going extremely well.

Late one afternoon, driving to catch the ferry back to the mainland I heard a commercial on the radio to remind us women to go and get our annual mammogram. Being under fifty I'd never had a mammogram. I thought, "I must get organized on this item too, why don't I book a mammogram." I called the toll-free number given out on the little infomercial and sure enough they had an appointment available in North Vancouver the next week. "Yikes, I'm not looking forward to that."

That weekend the kids and I had a fantastic time. I made spaghetti for dinner on Saturday night, they love my spaghetti as I don't put very many vegetables in it, but I do put in tons of garlic. After dinner I blasted the music and we cavorted and ran and played all around the house for an hour or so. This is one of the things I love doing with my kids, but unfortunately as they get older they don't like to spend as much time with me as they used to. Their lives now revolve around their friends, their social life and their iPods whereas my life still revolves around them. I understand their pulling away is all part of growing up and it's a process that every child needs to go through, although it still hurts when they say, "No mum I don't want to watch a movie with you. I want to watch movie with my friend". So for them to agree to cuddle up on the couch with me and watch a movie together that night was truly a blessing.

"Isn't this great you guys, family movie night" I said with a big grin on my face.

They looked at me with that "here we go again" look in their eyes. "Yes mummy" they said in unison.

"Can you make popcorn please mum?" Rose asked.

"No," I said with a sigh, "you already had dinner, and besides you didn't even finish your dinner you certainly don't deserve popcorn."

"Please mum," she said. "If Bob was here he let us have popcorn. I miss Bob mum, when is he coming home?"

"He'll be home in about three weeks, honey."

"That's just not fair mum, you got to see him in Australia, and we haven't seen him since the end of November." Rose complained.

"Yeah mum and then you guys are going to Texas so we won't even get to see him then," Kory said. "At least you could make us popcorn so we'd feel better and it would seem like he's here."

"You guys think you can sucker me that easily?" I asked.

"Yep," they both said, "so let's go make some popcorn."

"You win," I said on my way to the kitchen.

We stayed up way past my bedtime and theirs. By the time the second movie ended it was past midnight and I was exhausted. I chased them up into their rooms, threatened them with their lives if they woke me early, turned off the lights and we all went to bed.

Monday was a busy day. After dropping the children off at school, I drove to the city for our Monday morning meeting. We had a guest speaker this morning so the normally short meeting extended on until lunchtime. This gave me just enough time to deliver some paperwork in North Vancouver before I had to rush back up the highway again to get the children from school. It was a busy night, with soccer practice, swimming and dinner squished somewhere in between. The next morning I had to go back to North Vancouver, this time to the clinic for my very first mammogram. They did my right breast first. The technician forgot to check the calibration on the machine or something, but whatever it was that happened, the machine came down and with a squishing splatting feeling (like that when you squish a really FAT spider), my right breast was crushed. I screamed in pain and almost passed out. After I was normal again, she re-adjusted the machine and did the left side - lo and behold, hardly any pain.

I left there feeling traumatized and sore. Thankfully I had an office day scheduled so I didn't need to sit in front of people while in so much pain.

The next day, I got up early, still in a bit of pain, took some Advil, showered and drove to the ferry terminal. I had a busy two days on the coast ahead of me and needed to focus. The ferry ride was uneventful and in no time I was sitting in my office getting ready for my first appointment of the day. By two-thirty I was starving and in pain again. I took another Advil and went to Sushi

Bar Nagomi, the best Sushi restaurant on the Sunshine Coast.

Thirty minutes later, belly full, I was back in the office to finish up my day. It was a long afternoon, with my last client leaving at seven-thirty, and then I made the drive to mum's in Sechelt. Since she had already eaten earlier, we just sat in her room, drank tea and caught up on HGTV. I mentioned my sore breast and that the mammogram technician had basically admitted that she had made a mistake and instead of the machine stopping at a certain point, it went flat and crushed my little booby. We had a bit of a laugh imagining what might have happened if my boobs were really big, then we forgot about it and moved on to other subjects. My first appointment was very early the next morning to accommodate a shift worker, so I went to bed by nine o'clock.

Thursday I ran ragged all day and by the time I got on the ferry to head home at the end of the day, I realized I had barely eaten, let alone had any water all day. I walked up to the cafe in the ferry, stared at the gross food for a few minutes, and then bought only a bottle of water before heading back down to my car. Once the ferry docked, I called Ingo at Pepe & Gringo's to ask if he could prepare me some butter chicken and that I'd be there before they closed at ten o'clock.

Pepe's was quiet when I arrived. I sat at the bar and Ingo poured me a glass of wine before going to get my dinner.

"Thanks," I said with a sigh.

"Long day?" he asked.

"Yes, a long two days. I've been over on the coast and have been in meetings back to back for two days."

"At least you are keeping out of trouble," Ingo laughed.

"Trouble," I said, "I have barely the energy to eat right now, let alone get into any trouble. That's the problem when you take too many holidays. Returning to work you have to go into overdrive to catch up"

"When is Bob back?" he asked.

"In nine days, not that I'm counting. Then we leave for Texas on the twenty-fifth, and then two days afterwards is my birthday." I mumbled between bites of delicious butter chicken.

"Thirty-nine again?" Ingo remarked.

"Hell no, I'm too old to pull that off, I think. I'm going to own up to this one, it's my forty-seventh this year. I don't feel forty-seven and I don't think I look it, so why not flaunt it." I stifle a giggle as I say this.

Ingo pours me another glass of wine, gets one himself and joins me while I finish the rest of my meal.

I'm home by eleven, and let the dog out for a pee. He's happy to see me; dog sitters just aren't as good as his human mummy. After Waldo finishes his nightly sniff around the back yard, we go upstairs and climb into bed. It has been a busy but fruitful week, and I am now officially exhausted. Good night world.

The next morning when I awaken, my right breast is tender and there is a distinct golf ball size lump right in the middle. I get a call later that day to come in for a repeat mammogram. The weird thing is this repeat mammogram is on my left breast. They said my right one was fine, no signs of lumps or anything to be concerned about. I mentioned the pain and golf ball sized swelling. They said to talk to the technician when I came in for the second mammogram.

I am grateful for the weekend and some time to rest. It has been a long, busy week. Saturday is a quiet day with the children, and on Sunday I go for a long ride with Waldo. As we are hurtling down the trail in the woods I feel my right breast ache. This is ridiculous, now it is affecting my daily activity. I stop for a moment on the trail to try and get more comfortable, pretty hard to do with a sports bra on. "Arrgh," I think in frustration. This is ridiculous. "Come on Waldo, let's get home," on hearing the word home, he begins to bolt and off we go full speed ahead.

Later that evening as I am getting ready for bed, I notice that the nipple on my right breast has become inverted. This is just getting very weird. A huge, hard breast and an inverted nipple, the technician seriously did a number on me.

Finally it is March twenty-second, the day of my repeat mammogram for my left breast. I'm not looking forward to this and make a point of letting the technician know what happened to me last time and ask her to be sure to calibrate the machine properly. She looks at me like I am nuts. Then as she starts on the left, she notices the size of my right breast. It is hard to miss now, and is so enlarged that she has difficulty moving it out of the way to properly perform the mammogram on the left breast.

Thirty minutes later we are done and I'm sitting with the person who reads the results. "Good news," he says, "your left breast is clear, no cancer found."

"What about my right breast?" I ask.

"That was cleared last time," he says.

"Well, how do you explain this then?" I state, showing him my massive melon. "The technician crushed it with the machine when I was last here and now it's huge."

"Hmmm, it could be a bit of swelling and bruising from that, keep an eye on it, and if it isn't better in three weeks, then go and see your doctor," he says.

"Damn," I think as I walk out of there. I'm sick and tired of showing my breasts to these people. This is ridiculous. I bet if men had breasts they wouldn't have invented this type of squish test to check for cancer. Could you imagine if we put a man's balls through this. No way that would happen.

I get in my car feeling angry and frustrated. Oh well, I guess the good news is that I don't have breast cancer, it could have been worse. I turn the music up loudly and make my way onto the highway for the long drive home.

The next day Bob arrives home from Papua New Guinea. I am so overjoyed to see him. The kids are thrilled too as he comes bearing gifts, some cool statues and masks from Papua New Guinea. We spend two days doing laundry and preparing for our trip to San Antonio, Texas.

On Sunday the twenty-fifth we are up early and make our way to the Vancouver airport. It is a nice day in Vancouver but I cannot wait to get into the heat of Texas. After a long flight we finally arrive into the blazing Texan sun where we board one of the many shuttles to our hotel, the lovely JW Marriott San Antonio Hill Country Resort & Spa.

For four days we are treated like royalty. There are morning sessions where we get to hear about our colleagues' incredible successes and learn more about the business and then we have free time to spend by the pool or to shop for those who enjoy that. On one of the evenings we are transported out to a ranch for our own rodeo and huge Texan cook out dinner. The steaks were massive, as are most things in Texas. I had an opportunity to ride both a mechanical and a real bull as well as to hold an armadillo. After dinner a country band played live music and we danced until it was time to take the bus back to the resort. What an incredible evening.

The next day Bob and I spend by the swimming pool. We rent a cabana so we're not in the sun the entire time and spend half the time tubing down the huge waterslides and the other half lazing in the sunshine. On the following day we go into the San Antonio Riverwalk area with Daniel and Jacqueline. I really enjoy this area and on my next trip back to San Antonio would stay in one of the hotels along the river. The buildings are old with lots of character and the large old trees have been decorated with tiny LED's that make the entire area spectacular after dark.

The next day, Tuesday, is our last full day in San Antonio and also the evening of the Gala Ball. Bob and I are very excited for this evening and although I'm not a big fan of large sit down dinners, I do enjoy the social cocktail hour beforehand. The evening does not disappoint. Everyone is dressed to the nines and after dinner we are entertained by the spectacular LeAnn Rimes.

By the time we fly home on Wednesday we are both exhausted having been wined and dined for four straight days. Life is good.

## APRIL SHOWERS

As is typical, April starts out drearily. It's a grey Sunday morning, the kids are still asleep and even the dog doesn't want to go anywhere. Last week I was enjoying the Texas heat with Bob, and now I can feel the cold right through to my bones. Bob brings me a coffee in bed and I curl back under my quilt, wishing I could spend the entire day this way.

Soon enough though, the children are up wanting some of Bob's amazing pancakes and asking to be driven to friends' houses. I am having a hard time moving around because the pain in my breast is unbearable, so after I drop Rose and Kory off, I drive myself to the walk-in clinic.

I hate walk-in clinics, as there is always a long wait. Fortunately there is a Starbucks right next door, so I get myself a nice Latte, hook up to Wi-Fi and relax. Within no time, I'm called in and once again I have to expose myself to a doctor. Thankfully it is a female this time. She takes a look around and suggests I have mastitis. Mastitis, are you kidding? I thought that only happened when you are breast-feeding. Apparently I am misinformed. So, off I go with a prescription for antibiotics and a promise that all will be well in about a week.

One week later and I am standing in the pouring rain on a soccer field in Surrey watching Rose's game. Mum has come up for the weekend so she made the trek out with me. Rose has quite the family turn out to watch this tournament. My dad and his wife as well as my sister and her husband have both come out to watch and my brother Sean was also supposed to be here, but apparently he is running late. It is so cold and wet that we have to huddle together to keep warm.

Rose plays really well, they have two games today and finally at the end of the second game Sean arrives. She is ecstatic to see him. Sean is a huge bear of a man and Rose just loves to roughhouse with him. He also spoils her and Kory far too much for my liking, but when I complain he states plainly, "that's what uncles are for Michelle. Get used to it." Sean and I rarely see eye to eye, but he is my brother, and despite his stubbornness, I do love him. We walk a different path these days; so we don't see each other that often. However he always makes an effort where the kids are concerned. They are his only niece and nephew and he loves them dearly. After soccer the family gets together for coffee and hot chocolate before going our separate ways. It is a rare treat to all be together, and it makes me very happy.

Rose gets a ride home with her father, so it is just Bob and I driving back together. "Honey," I tell him, "there is really something wrong with my breast. The antibiotics haven't worked, it is still huge and now I can feel pain radiating under my armpit. I really think I need to go to the clinic again."

"Okay, let's go directly there then," he says.

Unfortunately it is Sunday so the clinic is closed, leaving the hospital emergency room as our only option. After a long wait I finally get seen. The doctor once again examines me and once again suggests mastitis. He decides to put me on two days of intravenous antibiotics. So I have to come into the hospital every twelve hours to get hooked up to an IV and they dose me. He also ordered an ultrasound of the breast to see what is going on.

On April eleventh, I get the results of the ultrasound. Results as per notes: The appearance of the breast suggests a degree of mastitis! Hello, we've already been here, but they don't listen. After two days of intravenous antibiotics, I am put on another seven-day dose of antibiotics.

I dutifully take all my medications and sure enough, nine days later I am back in the walk in clinic. The pain is now radiating under my armpit and up towards my neck. Also, a weird pink patch is on the right hand side of my breast, almost like a little bite. This doctor finally agrees with me. This is not mastitis. Perhaps it is fat necrosis. "What is that?" I ask.

"Well," he said, "if the mammogram crushed your breast and that killed the breast tissue, then we would see what is called fat necrosis, basically the tissue is dying."

"Wonderful, what do I do then?" I ask.

"If this is the case, we would probably need to go in and remove the dead tissue," he says.

"Seriously," I ask, "the damage from the mammogram is so bad that it might have killed the tissue, and now I'll have to get it surgically removed?"

"Perhaps," he says, "that is one of the possibilities. I'm going to refer you to a breast surgeon, they are the experts here."

So he gets on the phone to call a surgeon and I cannot believe what I am hearing on his side of the conversation. What it boils down to is this. The first surgeon he calls asks if it is cancer. My doctor says he doesn't know; that is why he is calling, so that I can be seen to determine what it is. The surgeon actually says to him, "If it is cancer, I will see her, if it is not cancer then I won't." Can you imagine that? Here we are, trying to determine what is wrong with my breast, and it could be cancer, yet the surgeon will not see me unless my doctor tells him for certain it is cancer. This is insane. If knew whom he had called, I would write him a nasty letter. Finally a Dr. Tree agrees to see me, the wait is ten days, but he will see me.

It has been over forty-five days since the horrible mammogram and finally someone is taking me seriously, but a ten-day wait? Bob and I shake our heads in frustration. There is still no relief for me other than instructions to take extra strength Advil for the pain. The rain is still coming down when we leave the clinic. April is almost over and I don't think we have had a single day without rain. It may be good for the plants, but it's certainly not good for my soul. I grew up in the southern hemisphere, I need light to survive, and at this rate I'll develop webbed feet. Please, bring on the summer and the brighter days.

## THE BOMB DROPS

As April turns into May there is finally a touch of warmth in the air. Beautiful pink blossoms are coming out on all the cherry trees and the streets look lovely. Bob has been working a lot in our backyard creating a little tropical paradise. The Tiki Bar is almost built and most of the huge decking has been put in. Once the weather warms up we will be putting the pool in. I cannot wait. Last year I loved swimming in the pool and this year we have a larger solar heater so it will be even better. The master plan is to create a backyard space that can be enjoyed by the whole family. There will be a swimming pool, hot tub, Tiki Bar, fire pit and dining/barbeque area. We started the project last summer and hope to have it complete this year. I am so lucky that Bob is not only handy, but he actually enjoys doing this type of work. The only challenges are time and money. Aren't they always the challenges of life?

Speaking of challenges, I have been having a hard time keeping up with my hectic work schedule because of the pain in my right breast. Not only is it exhausting me, but the amount of medicines I need to take to relieve the pain is also beginning to affect me. I finally saw the surgeon on May third. He suggested we do another ultrasound and schedule an MRI. He also said that if this was a hematoma or fat necrosis it should get better in the next few months. The second ultrasound revealed no changes so I am now waiting for the MRI. I am angry and frustrated. I cannot sleep for the pain, and my breast is now as big as a baseball and as hard as concrete.

Every second day I call to ask about an MRI date and get nothing. Finally my brother Sean and my friend Wendy intervene and start pulling strings at their end to get me booked in somewhere. Unfortunately, the hospital where Wendy's friend works does not do breast MRI's, however the friend did call Lions Gate MRI and pushed them to get me in.

Finally, all their pushing works. I get a call from Lions Gate to go in for my MRI on May twenty-ninth. I am so relieved.

Time literally crawls until the twenty-ninth. Finally the day is upon me. Bob drives me in to the hospital and we go down to the basement where the MRI machines are. I get to change into a beautiful blue hospital gown and wait in a little area until my name is called.

A rather robust nurse comes to get me and takes me down the hall to have an IV inserted so they can push dye into me during the MRI. I wasn't aware this was going to happen and warn the nurse that they will have problems with my veins. Of course she doesn't believe me, so after two futile attempts, the IV is still not in and they have to call a different nurse down to do it. By this point I am beyond distraught and just want to go home.

Presently the new nurse arrives. I look at her meekly. "Are you any good at this," I ask. She assures me she is an expert, looks at my veins, and shakes her head and goes to get a hot towel. Placing the towel on my lower arm she gives me a gentle pat on the hand. "Don't worry," she says in broken English, "I make easy for you." I smile and nod my head in agreement. At this point there is not much else I can do. She is however, true to her word and the needle slides in easily. She tapes the tubes and valves in place and I'm ready to go.

The MRI room is quite intimidating. The machine itself is huge. There are two technicians in there to help me get positioned. "Okay," the first one says, "we will get you to lie face down on the machine, then we will hook your IV up to our dyes." Weird I think as they lie me down, wriggle my right beast into this little cavity and hook me up to the dye. It is not exactly comfortable, but then again, this isn't the Ritz. The second technician explains that the MRI will take about forty-five minutes. They give me a headset to put on. Apparently the MRI machine is very loud so it is more relaxing to listen to music and block out the sounds. I am told that they will be able to hear me at all times, however if I am really panicked to squeeze this ball. I feel a small ball being placed in my hand. "Are you ready?" she asks.

"Yep," I say, worried that I might have an asthma attack or freak out from being trapped in a huge machine, "let's get this party started."

It is loud, unbearably loud and the headphones really do nothing to block it. I am told to relax and breathe normally as this thing whirs around my head like a spaceship. Clang, clang, whir, whir, bang, bang, whir, whir. Over and over again it goes. They keep checking in to make sure I am okay.  So far, so good.  Then they say it is time for the dye to go in.  It will burn going in, but only for about fifteen seconds, so don't worry about it.  It is easy for them to say.  In the dye goes, and it does burn, all the way up the vein but soon it is over.  The whirring and clanging continues, my arms ache from being positioned above my head and my sore breast is just yelling at me to get this over with.  It is with great relief that I hear them coming through the door.  "All done," they say in unison, "you did really well, and we got some great shots."

"Excellent," I say, "I'm pretty photogenic most of the time."

Off we go, back to Squamish and back to waiting.


It is a lovely Friday night; I'm out on my evening bike ride with Waldo and my husband and my cell rings.  It's a long distance number and I'm off work hours so at first I don't answer it.  Then eventually as it keeps ringing I am forced to.  It's the breast surgeon.  "Michelle, he says, it looks like you have Inflammatory Breast Cancer."

Silence

"What?" I ask.  "Are you kidding?  How can that be?  It must be a mistake?  This is damage from the mammogram, it has to be, how can it happen at the same time?  Something is just not right?"

"Sorry, he says, that is what the MRI technician has told me and so I've referred you to a special surgeon and Lions Gate."

"SHIT!"

I hang up the phone. Bob and Waldo are nowhere in sight as they continued on their ride when my phone call came in. Bob has no idea who it was on the other end of the line; otherwise, there is no way he would have left my side. I am only two blocks from home, but I don't know how to get there. I am so confused and so weakened by the news. I know I cannot get on my bike and ride, so I slowly walk, pushing it home. I am shaking, not from fear but from shock. How am I going to tell Bob? What does one say in a situation like this? What do I tell my family, my kids? This is so overwhelming. I never, ever thought I'd have to tell my family that I had a bad cancer. Not that any cancers are good, but some, like basel cell carcinoma are less life threatening.

I open the door to the house and call for Bob. He appears in the entryway and I break down, my words falling all over each other as I try to tell him about the phone call. We sit for a long time on the stairs in the hallway, Bob holding me and looking at me in disbelief as I relay to him the information I have just been given.

"Okay," I say to my Bob later that night over a bucket load of tears and confusion, "this must be a mistake." We'll go get that biopsy and see what's going on. Unfortunately I have to wait five whole days to get in to see the Doctor for the biopsy. Bob has to go out of town for work, so my sister Marie and my mother Jackie come up for a few days, mainly to keep me sane and also to act as a buffer with the children as I am finding it very hard to be around them right now. Telling mum and Marie is almost as difficult as telling Bob. I ask mum if she could tell my brother Sean for me, as I know he will have a fit and I cannot handle that right now. I am saved the pain of telling dad right now because he is in Paris on holidays. Telling dad and telling my children will be the hardest of all. I feel like I have failed my children. It is my job to raise them and I have no right to leave them while they are this young.

My thoughts over the next few days are all over the map. I meet with my dear friend Michele and tell her the news. I feel like a loser doing this. I am scared she won't want to be my friend anymore because now I have cancer. Cancer isn't cool; she can't be hanging with a bald cancer chick drinking champagne. That just doesn't jibe. She gives me a great big hug and we cry together. "I'm sorry," I say "I'm being silly. I am sure they have made a mistake, let's wait until the biopsy." All the while, I know in my heart it is true, and all the while I am worried she will abandon me for better, more alive friends.

I have been in tears for hours, have been laughing with mum about how I'll finally get to be a blonde and perhaps I'll get a nice tattoo on my bald head - oh and the best part, I can eat ALL I want now. I love food and have always watched what I eat. Now I don't need to worry about that.

Oh, but yes I do, because remember, this is all a big

mistake right!

Wrong.

On June fourth "C" Day, my friend Michele and her husband embark on their amazing trip to Europe and mum and I meet with the surgeon in North Vancouver. Nope he says after examining my breasts, lymph nodes, stomach, this is not fat necrosis, this is Inflammatory Breast Cancer (there's that stupid BIG word again), and it's spread to your lymph nodes and a small biopsy won't do and, and, and... ENOUGH ALREADY! I shut my mind. Blank, I'm just going to go blank. I'll do what he says... general anesthetic...blah blah... Lions Gate.... Thursday.... help... results... large piece biopsy.... what... nothing is registering. All I am thinking is sorry dear husband, sorry kids... sorry family...sorry.... I don't know what I did wrong? I've really screwed up now haven't I? How do I fix this one?

After the appointment mum and I go for sushi lunch and try to absorb what we have just heard. She is certain they have made a mistake and that everything will be okay. I don't know what to think so I just sit quietly and sip my tea. My phone rings, it is my brother Sean. He is hopping mad. "Michelle," he says, "Mum tells me you have cancer. Is this true? What's going on?"

"Yes Sean," I tell him, "it is true. I think I have Inflammatory Breast Cancer, they are going to do a biopsy to be certain."

"Oh, so it's only breast cancer, you'll be fine, what's the big deal?" he says. Sometimes Sean can frustrate the hell out of me.

"Yes Sean, it is breast cancer, and I will be fine, but it is a big deal," I tell him. "I have to go through chemotherapy and perhaps radiation and surgery."

"You'll be okay though," he says, and I realize that his harshness is his way of dealing with it, that he is worried, but cannot show it.

"Yes Sean, I will be fine," I reassure him. We say our goodbyes, I finish my lunch with mum and soon it is time to go. Mum drives to the ferry and I make the long drive up the highway. I am glad Bob is coming home tonight; I could not manage being alone right now.

It is still nice outside when I arrive home. Summer will be here soon, my favourite time of year. Little do I know that I won't be enjoying much summer sunshine this year. Today is my last day of somewhat normalcy. Soon I get the full diagnosis and prognosis. Right now, I think I'm going to drink some wine and relax in the sun with my lovely doggie.

## THIS MUST BE A NIGHTMARE

My first thought as I awaken from sleep is, this must be a nightmare.  Surely I just had a bad dream last night and imagined everything.  I give my head a shake and sit up.  Is this real?  I look at my phone, see the last few calls made over the past day or so, an incoming call from a long distance number and an outgoing call to my mother and know it has to be true.  Of course, it could still be a mistake.  They haven't done the biopsy yet and without that, it could all be errors in interpretation.

I get up, shower, brush my teeth and go down to my home office.  As I drink my coffee I open up a browser window and search Inflammatory Breast Cancer.  This is what I find:

*Inflammatory breast cancer or T4d tumours present with rapid development of swelling, redness and peau d'orange (skin edema), which is often mistaken for an infection and treated with antibiotics before the correct diagnosis is made.  A mass may be palpable or the breast may be diffusely involved.  The mammogram may show a discrete mass, but often there is only diffuse increase in density and skin thickening.  Although the diagnosis is primarily a clinical one, the distinctive pathological finding is the involvement of the dermal lymphatic vessels by tumour cells which results in the skin erythema and edema.  A biopsy (either core or open) to confirm the diagnosis should include skin for the examination of dermal lymphatics.  More extensive surgery is not part of the initial management.*

*Inflammatory breast cancer is the most aggressive form of breast cancer with a median survival of 18 to 24 months, despite intensive combined modality treatment leading to a high initial response.  Prompt initial referral to the BC Cancer Agency is suggested for these patients. Clinical trials are available and participation should be encouraged.*

*Inflammatory breast cancer should be managed like other inoperable locally advanced breast cancer (stage IIIB and C).*

Holy shit.  The first thing that I notice in all the technical speak is the survival rate is only one and a half to two years.  You must be kidding me.  I am too young for this, too young to die.  I sit at my desk in complete shock, tears streaming down my face.  I don't think I'm going to get very much work done today.

Sobbing, I wander into my husband's office. "Honey," I say, "I'm going to die.  I just read about IBC and it's deadly, and I'm going to die."

"No," Bob states emphatically.  "No, you are not going to die, I am not going to lose you.  We only just found each other and you promised you would grow old with me."  He hugs me and I feel his hot tears mix with mine.  I can taste the salt of them as my lips kiss his cheeks.  My heart is bursting in pain and reeling with shock. We hold each other tightly and slowly sink into his chair, our bodies heaving.

I don't know how long we sit like this, arms wrapped around each other, holding on for dear life and at a complete loss for words. It is as if the whole world has disappeared from around us. We hear no sounds other than the sound of our pain and eventually I become numb. I sit up looking into Bob's beautiful blue eyes. "I'm so sorry honey, so sorry to do this to you," I say. There are no more words, only immense sadness.

The next few days I am like a zombie. I go through the motions of living but really I am not. I am in a holding pattern. Nothing I do matters. I feel like a criminal out on bail. I know eventually I'm going to end up in the slammer and I'm just biding my time until that day.


Good morning surgery day. I know it is only a small surgery, but I'm not too psyched about it, especially since I haven't had anything to eat or drink – other than three ounces of coffee, since midnight and I'm bloody starving and getting really grumpy.

All things considered, I'm actually feeling pretty upbeat; I even dressed nicely for the occasion and washed my hair. Who knows when I'll be allowed my next bath. Unfortunately I cannot wear make-up, jewellery or deodorant/perfume, so I feel rather naked. I spend a few minutes in my office getting some work done, as I don't know what shape I'll be in when I get home. I have appointments scheduled for tomorrow that I'd like to attend, so best to have my ducks in a row.

This time tomorrow I could have a big chunk of my breast missing, but at least I'll still have my brain, at least most of it, and I'll be able to eat again. I'm so starving right now I could vomit! I want a big eggs benedict breakfast with lots of hash browns and sourdough toast loaded with butter...oh and followed by a mint milkshake! Yummy.

Well that's all for now. Time to hit the road. I take stock of myself as I leave home. I am a smiling, hungry, one hundred and twenty seven pound woman, still all in one piece. I wonder who will be coming home.

The drive to the hospital is uneventful and we get there at ten-forty five. Now I am bloody starving. I haven't eaten since about eleven o'clock last night and I have to admit I had too much wine with my girlfriends. So all I want right now is a greasy breakfast and some good coffee. Bob knows I cannot go without food for a few hours without getting a bit snarly, so he is very patient with me. They ask me to change into a lovely gown, lovely if you are partial to blue polyester, which I am not, so it is not making me happy.

Finally after another thirty minute wait, they hook up my IV and roll me into the OR. By this time I am extremely dehydrated and am tired of the questions the nurses ask me over and over again. I just want this to get started. I have been pretty brave up until now when suddenly the whole fear of going under and never seeing my family again really hits me. Surrounding me are two nurses, two anesthetists and my doctor. They know I am upset and speak to me kindly. One of the anesthetists begins explaining what they were going to do - give me oxygen and then gently slip me under with drugs in my IV. "Do you have any questions?" he asks.

"Please don't kill me." I say, wondering what he thinks of that odd statement, but he is pretty cool looking as I fade away into oblivion.

I awaken two or so hours later crying in pain and actually crying for my mummy. Funny how even at forty-seven we never forget that the person who cared for us most was our mother. A lovely nurse comes over, holds my hand and gives me more pain medication. This process, me waking up crying for my mum and for the pain to go away goes on for an hour or so until they manage to give me enough pain meds. Then I drift off to La La Land.

Dr. Que, the surgeon, comes in at some point and speaks with me. He says he did find some "bad stuff", whatever that means, and so he sent the sample to a different lab to get more detailed results. So that means a longer wait and what the hell is "bad stuff"? I know this is all a big mistake, it's just a massive bruise and I'm going end up with a lovely new booby afterwards...so don't tell me about bad stuff.

Around four o'clock the nurse comes in and tells me I can get ready to go home. She starts to help me get dressed, "uh oh, this isn't so good," and the minute I sit up nausea starts. She declares me not ready to go back home yet and gives me a lovely shot in the butt as I lie here with a brown disposable basin trying not to hurl all over their bedding.

Eventually however, I ask for Bob and he tells them I feel capable now of going home. Bob and the nurse transfer me to a chair and wheel me to the car where I collapse into a ball on the front seat. He then covers me with a blanket from the hospital and off to sleep I go.

Twenty-four hours later, here I am. Step one of one hundred is now complete. It's funny, this is what I told my daughter when she went to her first audition. I said "Honey you will need to do at least one hundred auditions before you'll get hired for your first job."

I feel like I'm walking the same long path to something, I have no idea what is in store for me. I lie here in bed daydreaming about how I'd love to share my story on "W" or "Life" network. I think it would be an interesting one, imagine them following me through all these hurdles. Yesterday would have been a funny one as I was completely out of it with all the drugs they gave me. Perhaps, I think, this is all happening so I can finally fulfill my life long dream to act. Ha Ha Ha.... okay, calm down Michelle, I must still be on drugs.

I don't recall the ride home. I do recall being brought a lovely pink Popsicle in bed and apparently I had all kinds of conversations last night with Bob, but I don't remember any of them.

Today I am still a bit drugged up, but have to go to see two clients later this afternoon, so I have stopped the narcotic pain meds for a while and have taken extra strength Tylenol (because I am going to need the extra strength to pull off these meetings). Bob will drive me and wait for me at both appointments as I am in no state to be operating any machinery today.

Finally, the long day is over. Bob and I get home from my client appointments and he asks what I'd like to do for dinner. I'm too tired to decide yet so I suggest we enjoy the last few rays of sun in the backyard for a while. Just as I sit down, the phone rings. It is Dr. Que. He begins speaking and suddenly it is as if the world stands still. I can't find any words, I can't even move. I just listen and keep saying, "are you sure", "are you really sure?"

Yes, he says as gently as he can. I'm sorry Michelle but the test results are conclusive, you have Inflammatory Breast Cancer.

BOMB DROP!  SILENCE!

I'm too shocked to know what to do, too shocked to ask what stage it's at or what's next.

He did tell me that it's either stage III or stage IV as it has already spread into my lymph nodes. I also know that I'm about to be referred to an Oncologist whose primary role is to try to stop this cancer from eating me up alive - which it appears to be doing pretty rapidly. However the current method of stopping this cancer from killing me is to fill my body with all kinds of poisons that will make me wish I really would die.

The night is very hard for Bob and me.  I think this is harder for him than it is for me because he has to take care of me and watch me wither away, not a nice experience to go through.  I am trying hard to keep strong because this evil just wants me to be weak.  There are moments however that aren't that easy.

I take something to help me sleep and awake at five o'clock Saturday morning just sobbing.  Deep chest heaving sobs, throbbing though out my whole body.  I am going to die!  I've been given my walking papers.  I always said that if I knew I was going to die I'd do all the things I want to do and live to the fullest until that happens but I am so weak now that I cannot even imagine biking around Europe with my girlfriends (which is what I wanted to do for my fiftieth birthday).  Chemo is going to suck what little energy I have left right out of me so just how the hell am I going to get all this done.  I get out of bed and write my list.

My wishes before I die:

I promised the kids I would make 'Convention' again this year at work and take them on the Cruise in April 2013, and take them and Bob to South Africa my homeland

I want to take the family to Europe.

I want to take them to New York City.

The children want to go to Disneyland.

I want to go to Hawaii.

I want to go to Las Vegas with the kids and Bob.

I want to see the back deck completed and swim in our pool next summer and have a big summer bash.

I want to see my children graduate and get married and have babies.

I want to live a long, long time and grow old with my husband.

I just want to continue to work hard and enjoy my job and my family and pretend this never happened.

It's Sunday morning and I'm up early again, four days before I see the oncologist. This is my life now. Everyday I wake up with the knowledge that I am damaged. I am a ticking time bomb and nothing I can do will change that. All the little things that were so important just don't matter anymore. Nothing much does except for my family. We told the children last night. It was very difficult, and after some initial tears from Rose it was all over. They seem to be adjusting well, but then I think it will not really affect them until they see me actually ill. Life is going on as normal around me and I feel almost as if I am in another dimension. I go through the motions of eating pancake breakfast, riding with the dog, making the kids grilled cheese sandwiches for lunch, but I'm not really here, not really connected. Every few hours I hide myself in my bathroom as the grief overwhelms me and I cannot stop the tears from coming. Then I go back into the fray and it's as if nothing has changed.

Bob makes homemade pizza for dinner tonight, a

family favourite. The kids are laughing and joking as usual, with Kory doing his usual dinnertime comedy routine. I am happy inside as I realize that even without me, they will be okay. They will adjust and their lives will go on, and they will laugh again. I am just so sad that I will miss it all.

I sit up and give myself a mental kick. This is ridiculous; I have to stop this line of thought. I know the statistics are bad, but I've never allowed myself to be a statistic and I'm not going to now. I stand up to clear the dishes. "Who wants dessert?" I ask. Silly question, I realize as I leave the room to the sounds of "me, me, me."

It is a school night so the children and I are in bed by nine-thirty. I'm exhausted and hope that I will finally get a good night's sleep. I doesn't take me long to drift off.

"Mum, mum," I hear Rose crying from her room. I look over at the clock; it is ten past two in the morning. I climb out of bed and walk down the hallway to her bedroom.

"I'm here love. Everything's okay, mummy is here," I say, getting under the covers and holding her in my arms.

"No mum," she said, "it's not okay. You are going to die and I'm scared mum. I'm scared I'm going to be all alone and there will be no one to cuddle me like you do."

I don't know what to say. Tears are now running down my face as well. I hug her tighter "I'm here baby girl, I'm here". We cry together in each other's arms. As

I start to drift off to sleep she gives me a little shake. "You're all twitchy mum," she says.

"Sorry honey, I'm falling asleep, are you okay now?" I ask. She nods yes so I tuck her nicely in and go back to my room. Of course, now I cannot sleep.

Then it hit me. I am helpless. I am standing here on the shoreline looking out into the ocean at the biggest wave you have ever seen. I know it is going to come crashing down with such force it may possibly kill me in the process. However I cannot move. I am transfixed. I have the knowledge - "you have IBC". I know some of the facts - "I have to go through chemo", "I'm going to lose my hair" etc. but to know it and fully live and embrace it are two completely different things.

No wonder I am so calm now (well mostly). I have no reference point for this, nothing with which I can measure what is about to hit me. I mean yes, the pain at the incision in my breast from the biopsy hurts, but how does that compare to the pain of having both breasts removed and all the tissue along my ribcage and in my lymph nodes? How painful is that going to be? Not just the physical pain but also the mental anguish too. I have always identified myself as a sexy cute little thing, not that my breasts have ever been spectacular, but they were part of this feisty little package that drew people to me. My hair too, my hair which is now finally all I want it to be, long and soft and beautiful, will all be gone. I'll probably have a crew cut then be bald. I will be the ultimate little punk chick, bald and with no breasts. I am not sure that I will embrace that. I cannot even imagine that right now except in the far off impossible sense. I suppose I could bring out the funky clothes and attitude to match - who says I'm too old to dress like a punker.

And then there is Chemo, this I am terrified of. Again, I cannot even imagine it. I have read some blogs about what it feels like, but to actually put my body and soul through it and to sit watching my husband suffer as he holds my hands to help me go through it, the thought is too much to bear. I hear that your body burns up for days and that the nausea is like having a burning acrid rock in your stomach. I am afraid of this. No, I am terrified, but I'll have to go in for months with my hankie on my head and my body getting skinnier and greyer and sit with this poison dripping into me all so I can fight this stupid ASSHOLE who decided to shit on my parade. I am so scared. I am going to be such a burden to my family and I hate that. Don't get me wrong, I love being catered to, when I am cute and sexy and can smile back and say "thanks for the coffee honey", not when I can barely lift my head off the pillow and I smell like disease and medicine, no, this I do not want.

My father always said "Michelle, life isn't fair, it's how you deal with it that counts" and he was right, as he always is, but hell this just SUCKS and I know I'm supposed to learn something from this, or that there is some reason why I have this, I just can't seem to find that. What good does it do giving a mother of two young children a devil like this to fight off? Have I not loved my family enough? What should I have done differently? It's all so pointless to ask or think these things because it's just RANDOM. My number just came up and I have to stand tall and take the shit that's going to come, and that massive wave is getting closer and I still have no idea how I will manage to fight my way back to the surface and live through it, but bloody hell I'm going to swim and fight and try with every fiber of my being.


Today is Monday...today I can still work. Today is another day of not really knowing - and I am glad for that. Although I have been up now for hours, the sun is just now beginning to rise over the eastern range. I know I should get up and start making school lunches and pancakes, but I'm just not ready for it. "Isn't this the last week of school before summer holidays?" I ask myself as I drag my butt out of bed. Oh well, a mother's life never slows down. I look at myself in my bathroom mirror. I don't look like I'm dying. My eyes are swollen from not having slept very much but other than that I look completely normal. My beautiful long hair is shiny and healthy, and my skin, although sporting a few wrinkles these days, looks pretty good. No one would take me for a day over forty, let alone forty-seven and raging with cancer cells.

I keep looking into my eyes and I see the eyes of a little girl looking back at me, the little me, the Michelle that was once as free as a bird. I see images of myself as a child running around our property in South Africa or jumping off the diving board into the swimming pool. So young, so carefree, I had my whole life ahead of me. This little girl looks back at me pleading, almost begging for this to be a mistake. I feel my heart ache as I tell her how sorry I am. Little one, I say, I'm so sorry I didn't hold up my end of the bargain and give you the adulthood you always wanted and deserved. I'm so sorry that you are not going to get a chance to grow old and experience all the other joys of life that we have yet to find together. She is crying now too, I hug her and hold her close to my heart. Sorry, sorry I sob.

A knock at the door alerts me. It's Bob asking if he can make the pancakes for the kids. He is such a blessing. I clean up my face, wait a few minutes until any evidence of crying is gone and go downstairs to start on the school lunches.

Monday and Tuesday are very difficult days. I try my best to work, but find I've had to cancel my client meetings for fear of breaking down in front of the client. I sit quietly in my office most of the day doing paperwork and waiting for night to come so I can sleep and get some peace.

Tomorrow I meet with the oncologist to find out my fate. I think until then this is all pretty unreal. I have noticed some subtle changes, like not having enough energy to make it through most of the day without a nap, feeling exhausted deep in my core and an overwhelming sense of grief, pain or regret building up inside of me. I'm not sure what it is and I stop it when it tries to pour out because I am worried I will lose complete control.

Today I spend most of the day with Rose, we drive to Vancouver for a doctor's appointment and it takes all my strength not to break down on the way in. She asks me a little bit about my cancer but she doesn't really understand. She asks if I am going to die. What do I say to that one? I say I don't know, it just doesn't make sense to me to tell her that no I won't, because that wouldn't be fair to her. Kory seems to just be ignoring the entire thing, perhaps that's his way of dealing with it, but it breaks my heart when he is rude to me because in the back of my mind I am thinking "hey I might not always be here, love me dammit"! I just want to sit them both down and tell them to be kind to each other and be kind to me because pretty soon life will be very, very hard and they will need each other.

In the past few days some amazing people have reached out to me to provide me with support. Their thoughts and suggestions, especially about support groups and nutritional websites have been very helpful. I got a great email from a woman who has offered to help me to pick out a good wig, should I choose to go that route when my hair falls out. I was so excited because I have the perfect Marilyn Monroe style in mind, although, Rose has suggested I cut my hair very short first and dye it all sorts of colours. This could be fun.

The books and nutritional references have been very informative; I guess I'm going to end up a Greens Freak after all. I even had fresh Arugula in my shake this morning. Bob has been amazing, providing foods that he knows are good for me and holding me when I have my mini breakdowns. Last night was quite funny - in hindsight of course - because I had a terrible nightmare about Death (he didn't have a scythe, but was more of a black shadow with a sombrero style hat) coming to get me in my bedroom, and in my dream Bob wasn't waking up so I started screaming to wake him up. Apparently I was screaming so loudly that I really did wake him up. He said that in all the times I've had nightmares, he's never heard me scream that strongly and that loudly. I'm going to remember that for when I have bad days ahead, scream with force and kick the devil out of me.

Wednesday, Oncologist Day, and I am in a good mood this morning. Wearing my city duds I arrive at Lions Gate Hospital promptly at nine-thirty (dad always told me to never be late), to find out that they have no record of my appointment with Doctor Sasha.

"Excuse me?" I ask, shocked. "What do you mean no record of an appointment with Sasha?"

The receptionist looks at me rather sheepishly. "Who referred you?" she asks.

I am steaming now. "Dr. Que referred me, he did the biopsy," I declare with gritted teeth.

You mean to say we sped all the way down here to get here on time for nothing? So we wait and we wait. I call Dr. Que's office to tell them what's going on - get an answering machine and finally a call back from a women who herself hasn't a clue. So here I am, sitting in Oncology, which really sucks. You have no idea. I mean, it's hard enough going to a cancer ward and seeing all these terribly ill people if you are just visiting, but to go there and see them and know you are one of them, well, that's just impossible to grasp. I am trying so hard to be brave but every time I see someone who is bald or green/grey from all the illness and chemo, well I just break down.

So...where am I? Oh yes, here we are, Bob and I sitting here. Me, crying occasionally, ever so quietly on his shoulder, and Bob sitting with steam coming out of his ears. To know Bob is to know a man who never gets angry, and I mean never. He's the most gentle, calm person you can ever meet. I hardly recognize him today, he is all Alpha male and pissed right off that I "a Cancer Virgin" has to sit here in this situation and see it all.

Finally an hour after waiting - I know that's not long for most people, but I'm anal about being on time and anal about not waiting - a lady calls us to go half way down the hall to sit and wait for Sasha. That throws me over the edge. Half way down the hall gives us a clear view of everyone in the beds and chairs hooked up to their chemo treatment. It is so sad, so devastating and so unreal. I can't look, I can't move. "This can't be real, this can't be for me," I think. "Why am I here?" No seriously, this must be a joke. Cancer is only a word, right? It's not real and it really cannot be happening to me. However it is, as much as I still don't understand or realize it, it is. Thankfully this lovely women who took us "half way down the hall" realizes I am a "Cancer Virgin" and sees the effect this is having on me and takes us directly into the examining room (ahead of a poor little gentleman). Then the information overload starts.

Sasha is fabulous, young, informed, kind, just the best kind of doctor you could want in this situation. He is very direct -I think because I present myself as someone who wants "direct, no holding back, give me the shit" kind of information. He spends an hour and a half with us.

The results of the biopsy are positive for cancer in the breast skin tissue, positive for cancer in the breast itself and positive for cancer in the lymph nodes. The cancer is Inflammatory Breast Cancer - read Cancer on Steroids - or as he said Advanced Breast Cancer. It is rare (less than one percent of all breast cancer patients have this), it is frigging aggressive and it's eating away at me. Me, with this body that I've tried all my life to make as good as it can be. I mean I didn't watch all my food and exercise and all that bull for nothing.

Yikes, so I'm taking this all in and my mind is reeling - but I'm listening, yep I'm listening, keep spewing, keep throwing this at me. I'm strong right. So, the good news is, it's Estrogen Negative, phew and it's HER2 positive. "How is this good news?" I ask.

"Well," Sasha says, "with HER2 positive IBC I have a good chance of surviving. It has a specific type of treatment and it's a better diagnosis than if it were not HER2 positive." That doesn't sound too encouraging to me, but I guess one takes every single thing as positive at this point.

"Michelle," Sasha says, "you need to know that if you don't start chemotherapy and hit this cancer hard, you will not be with us by Christmas."

"Are there other, less harsh treatments I can do?" I ask.

"No, with this type of aggressive cancer we need to hit you very hard with chemotherapy, then after that is complete, we will send you for radiation therapy, and then after that is done, we hope that the cancerous mass is manageable enough for us to operate and you will have a mastectomy," Sasha says.

"However, that being said, we don't know yet if the cancer has spread to other parts of your body. So, before we even go any further you need to have a CT Scan." Sasha states, like this is a common daily occurrence for me.

Since the CT is urgent, and because this cancer asshole is eating away at me as I sit there, Sasha, with all his magic power arranges for me to have the CT Scan within the hour. Once that is arranged, he continues on with further information about treatment and things I need to know. Suffice to say that half of it goes in my mind, the other half flies overhead as I sit there looking at him thinking, you've got this wrong. I'm too young, I totally rock at loving and living life, and this has to be a mistake. Then the other side of me, the nasty little guy sitting on my shoulder is saying, perhaps you deserve this. Perhaps you aren't kind enough or grateful enough, perhaps you need to be humbled, you didn't live the right life and now you're going to have to learn the hard way. Damn my Catholic guilt is kicking in. Oh well, I'm on the elevator to hell now, next stop CT Scan.

Down we go to radiology where I get into the lovely clothes again and sit and wait for my scan. I sit next to a lovely lady and her husband and I'm still living the life, you know, happy "it's all good" kind of life. She asks if "I have to drink the liquid?"

"No," I say, "no one gave me a liquid."

She says, "you're lucky, it tastes awful, and I have to drink three glasses of it."

"Oh, what are you here for," I ask, regretting the question as soon as it leaves my mouth.

"I have had Colon Cancer for six years, and it's come back again," she says in a calm, quiet voice.

"I'm sorry," I say and smile.

Six years I sit there thinking. How horrible, if I could kill cancer I would. I wouldn't be nice about it either. It would be a horrible, nasty, long process and I'm sure thousands of people would join me. I mean what did mankind do that we deserve such hell, and not just the people who get cancer, but what about the families who have to support us. I feel like such a failure getting this,

I'm supposed to be the strong one; I'm not supposed to burden my family with this. Oh well, shit happens right, so off I go to get my scan. They put in an IV for the dye, now this is interesting. I had a CT Scan about twenty-five years ago, when I had a lot of migraines, and I do recall the dye, but I certainly don't recall the side effects. Perhaps it is because they are different now. What I do recall is back then in the olden days, the CT Scan machine didn't speak to you. Yep, he speaks to you. The technician neglected to mention that, and after having an MRI last week, which is far worse than a CT Scan, I was not expecting this. Then you lie on a bed that slides into a tubular shaped machine and they hook your IV line up to two huge syringes on the side - don't worry Michelle, we will come in and let you know when we're putting the dye in - okay, so nothing to worry about, then this automated guy suddenly shocks the hell out of me and says "Breathe in", "hold your breath." Oh hell, I guess I'd better. I hope he tells me when to breathe again. So I breathe in, I hold and hold and finally he thankfully says, breathe. Phew! He repeats his instructions over and over and I'm very obedient, I breathe in, hold, and breathe out. Then the technician comes in and says, "We're going to inject the dye now, it's going to burn as it goes up your arm, it's going to make you get hot all over and it's going to make you feel like you have to pee, but that's okay, you won't pee, really I promise you won't, it will just feel like you have to." Wow, that's comforting. "Oh well," I say to myself, "this is nothing compared to what's going to happen to me in the next few months, so just lie here and think of Mexico."  So I do, and it's all fine, really - although I did get all hot and bothered.  However, it's all over in no time and off we go back to Oncology to meet with the nurse.

The nurse sits with me to explain all about chemotherapy.  I am overwhelmed; I cannot take any of this in.  Thankfully she hands me a folder with pages upon pages of notes for me to take home and read at my leisure. Sasha pops in with some good news, "The cancer has not spread to other parts of my body – well ninety-nine percent certain, and they will monitor that.  Oh and by the way, you start Chemo tomorrow," he says.

"Excuse me?"

"Yes, it's serious, it's a rush.  We cannot wait, so we start tomorrow and it's going to be a great cocktail, you're really going to love it," the nurse says with a smile. "We're going to give you four drugs via intravenous for four hours a day, every three weeks for eight cycles. – In other words, six months.  Then we only give you one drug called Herceptin for the remaining nine months."  It's called ACDT protocol, but all I heard was this.

Drug # 1 - The hair loss, nausea and mouth sores drug - but really we'll give you more drugs to counteract that.  Oh and it can cause heart failure, so please sign this waiver.

Drug #2 - Diarrhea and burning on urination drug - oh it's not so bad and if it gets very bad, take Imodium.

Drug #3 - The nerve damage and crazy nails drug -

we promise, you will get your feeling back in a year or so, but you may have chemo brain!

Drug #4 - Oh yeah more heart problems and leg swelling - I thought chemo was supposed to make you skinny?

Then after each session I get an injection that is supposed to help my immune system get stronger, because it's kind of dead now after all the poison that has been pushed into it. This injection costs two thousand and seven hundred dollars per injection. Did I hear that correctly, two thousand and seven hundred dollars per injection? The way I calculate that is around forty-seven thousand dollars just for that injection alone, which is not covered by BC Medical, but may be covered by my group plan. This is on top of all the prescription drugs that I have to take that thankfully are covered eighty percent by my benefit plan and the natural medications I need to take to heal that are not covered by any benefit plan. Cancer is an expensive proposition. We never hear that side of the story now, do we?

After a long, mentally draining day we finally leave the hospital with a promise to be back first thing in the morning to start my chemotherapy. My mind is reeling; this is all happening far too quickly.

Bob pulls into the driveway and I hop out. I am exhausted, raw and shocked and really cannot think straight. I open the door and what I see has me in awe and so honoured and so proud. My beautiful daughter had asked her entire two grade five classes to get involved in a project and they had made this huge card for me. It was sitting on the stairs and was the first thing I saw as I walked in the door. The front of the card was all about "boobies" and "I love boobies" and the inside of the card had a group photo of each class. Everyone, including the principal and the teachers, signed it. I could not believe she had done this. I am so blessed by her generosity, her love and her joy and everything that little bundle of love has inside her. Now that is love.

I pick up the phone to thank her. "I'll hang it on my bedroom wall," I say.

"Do you really like it Mum," she asks?

"Honey, it's the most special, beautiful thing you could ever imagine. Thank you so much. I love you to bits," I say.

"I love you more" Rose says

"Nope, I love you more," I say

We both laugh. This is an ongoing joke with us and sometimes we can both continue for ten minutes arguing who loves whom more. "I know it's early, but I have to go because I'm going to go to bed now honey," I said.

"Okay mum, good night, I love you." She says.

I hang up, drag myself up the stairs to my bedroom, strip down beside the bed, climb in under the covers and am out before my head hits the pillow.

## I WISH I WAS DEAD

Thursday morning. Thursday June 14th, 2012. It is my first chemotherapy day and the day I have to break the news to my father. I wake up happy as I do most mornings, the middle of the night tears gone, but this is a unique morning, as many have been in the past week. I have my shower, still singing, and then think, "Hmmm, today is a big day. What does one wear for Chemo?" Something comfortable I would imagine, something not too flashy, certainly no jewellery, oh and what of my lovely "virgin showing" hair? Well I won't have that for much longer, so I'll wear it down and shiny. No make up of course, too many tears are going to flow this day, but what girl can go anywhere without her perfume? Today I choose a new one, "Vetiver of Haiti" by "The 7 Virtues Fragrance Collection". Bob brings me a lovely cup of coffee and has even learned how to make my protein/greens shake, so as I dress for the slaughter, he chats to me and makes sure I am fed. All in order to keep my pecker up and stay strong for today. I bring a great book to read, my Mac to work on and a list of all pain relievers I had taken overnight. I am ready to get on this horse.

The long drive to the hospital is a bit rocky, I get car sick, which is not what you want prior to chemo, and I am beginning to get very scared and a little sad. I am trying so hard not to cry throughout all this because it only makes others cry and this is not their burden. Bob has a hard enough time keeping his own career going and looking after my physical needs, he doesn't need the burden of my emotional needs. We get to the chemo ward just on time and go to the nurses station at the back. They are expecting me, and my lovely long hair is a dead give away. They are also ahead of the game and know about the medication that I was originally prescribed and which I am allergic too.

They ask me to lie in the bed right across from the nursing desk. The strong me immediately decides she's going to fly the coop or go hang in the lobby and people watch. It is because suddenly there I am staring at this stark white bed with all the machines and I think, there has got to be a mistake. Surely this is a joke, but no, the nurse Gabi, sees my distress, gets me into a sitting position on the bed and speaks to me very kindly. "You will be okay," she says. "I will be your nurse and I'll sit with you and we will get you through it. I will explain everything before it happens and what you are to expect."

It takes an hour to mix my chemo medicines in a closed lab. They don't do this until you get here because the medicines are so toxic and expensive and they don't want the technicians to mix them for no reason. So Bob and I sit and do the crossword. Another nurse comes in and puts in the IV line, they use this to provide the two types of chemotherapy drugs that I am getting today. One is pushed in through a valve via a massive and I mean massive needle, the other is dripped in over the course of an hour through the IV.

A half hour later the nurse comes by with a huge load of medication for me to take. Pills for nausea (lots and lots of those), a pill for skin rash...that sounds gross, and a pill to calm me down, I guess they've noted I'm a little freaked out right now and I imagine I need to be calm for all of this. A few other pills to prevent certain allergic reactions, by this time most have gone over my head. Finally I'm beginning to calm down. Gabi comes over and introduces me to the girl who is sitting to the left of me.

She is a lovely, soon to be 43 year old South African woman who at the age of 39 got Inflammatory Breast Cancer, but they found it so late that they also found it in her liver. It had already metastasized. Her story certainly put me in my place. She was happy, pretty, had short hair and was there with her mother and father. She was the main breadwinner of the household and for the past three and a half years has not been able to work as she went through her treatment. The worst was that the doctors gave her the wrong drug at the very beginning, which put her into intensive care, and then eventually she was put on life support and into a coma, however her mother was strong like a bull. When they said that her daughter might never come off life support or live a proper life again, her mother kept saying, "No way! Not my daughter." And here they are today, four years later, and she is alive and well. She still has to come in for Herceptin IV every three weeks for the rest of her life and they keep having to have PT Scans to see if the cancer has spread anymore, but for now, she is living. She is back working now, twenty-two hours a week is really all she can handle, but she is now supporting her family again and she says that there are mostly good days ahead.

I cannot thank them enough for their story and hope to see them again every three weeks. Being a South African myself attracted me to speaking to them in the first place, but to hear their battle and their courage and their happiness now is just wonderful.

So here comes beautiful Romanian Gabi. "Are you ready now", she asks gently "Ready as I'll ever be and thank you for the introduction to my roommate."

Gabi smiles, "We are going to start now with the bright red radioactive drug. I will sit with you for about twenty to thirty minutes while I slowly push the drug into your vein and watch for any allergic reaction." I don't watch. I turn and hold Bob's hand and we have mundane conversation most of which I will certainly forget, but he is here and he holds my hand and it is good. A few little tears shed, nothing more.

Later my roommate comes back, all smiles. Her PT Scan is clear, the family is ecstatic, all smiles and happy. Dr. Sasha suggests they go out and have a bottle of champagne after the Herceptin has been administered, but she just wants to go shopping. I am thrilled for her and give them all a big hug when they leave.

Soon Gabi is back with the IV drip of the next

exciting cocktail I am to have today.    "Where's the champagne," I am thinking.    However truly I think I'd throw up any alcohol that came near me right now.    This one she hooks up to the IV line and sits with me for a few minutes watching for any reaction.    When it looks like all is good, I send Bob off to eat and I go to sleep for a while. It's not a very restful sleep as the counsellor comes around to talk to me, which is nice, although I'd rather sleep.    She tells me about support groups that I will need to get through this and the yoga days etc.    I know it will be important later, but I am a rather private person (don't particularly like group activities and like to make my own friends), so for now this is hard to get excited about.    She is very kind and eventually realizes that I'd rather be sleeping and takes her leave.

At around one o'clock Bob is sent to the pharmacy for more drugs for me to take home and by one thirty a green zombie machine and her lovely handsome husband are on their way home.    It's almost like coming home from the hospital with a new baby.    Bob must have wondered who mixed up his baby with a green Martian baby. Weird.

I sleep almost the entire way home and go directly to bed when I get there.    After a few hours of something resembling sleep I wake up remembering that I need to call my father.    I am afraid to make this call, afraid to tell him that his daughter has cancer.    He always had such hopes for me, and now I'm going to let him down by telling him that I have cancer and I'm going to die before he does. The worst pain in the world has to be having your children die before you do, and I'm inflicting that on both my parents. The guilt I feel is tremendous. Thankfully, he is not yet home from Paris, so I leave a voice mail asking him to call when he is back and rested.

Bob tries to bring me some soup to eat, but I cannot bear the smell of cooked food. I drink a large glass of cold water and go back to bed. I'm feeling terrible, I drift in and out of sleep and a few hours later am awakened by Bob. "Your dad is on the phone," he whispers. I bolt upright and stare at him holding the phone, too afraid to take it. Bob gently puts it into my hand and I begin speaking.

"Hi dad, how are you?" I ask. "How was Paris?"

"Fine thanks love, just a little jetlagged, how are you?" he asks.

"Um, well, I have something to tell you dad. It's bad. Are you sitting down?" I say.

"Yes," he says, although I doubt that he is.

"Dad, dad, I'm really sorry," is all I can manage as I burst into tears.

"What is it dear?" he asks. I can hear the worry in his voice.

"Dad…I have cancer." I say.

Silence.

"I'm so sorry dad. I'm sorry I have disappointed you and failed you." I say.

"Darling, quiet now, there is no need to apologize," he says. "Are you okay?"

"Well, I had my first chemo today, so I'm in pretty rough shape, but I guess I'm okay" I say. "I'm sorry daddy."

"Love, give us a few days to get settled and then we will come up and see you. How about on Sunday?" he asks.

"Yes," I sob, "Yes Sunday will be fine, I'm not going anywhere."

"Okay, we'll see you then," he says.

"I love you dad, " I say.

"I love you too Michelle. Goodbye," and he is gone.

The next few days are pretty horrific. I will save the details, suffice to say, the poison is running though my veins and into every cell in my body. I am exhausted beyond belief, one minute I'm burning up, the next minute my pajamas are soaked through with sweat. My urine is burning red and I am drinking bucket loads of water at the doctor's recommendation. Bob spends Thursday at home with me, but then on Friday morning he has to go to work for a few days. My friend Wendy stops by at some point, I have a vague recollection of her sitting in the chair beside my bed, but otherwise, her visit is a blank. Chantal stops by on Thursday to see what I need, and when I wake on Friday morning, she is downstairs cleaning the fridge and putting in small portions of healthy soups, fresh cut fruit and vegetables and all the goodies a person going through chemo could need. Chantal, you are a godsend. A short while later Arlene arrives with a bevy of fresh tropical fruit, all cut in perfect portions to make it easier for me.  I am so overwhelmed by this expression of love from a friend I only knew for a short period of time, I do not know how to respond.

Mum arrives just as Chantal was leaving - perfect timing because being alone right now is a little difficult, and I need to be at the hospital in fifteen minutes for the Neulasta shot that I have to get.  Remember the two thousand and seven hundred dollar shot I need after each chemotherapy session to help bring my white blood cells up to normal.  The one that causes serious side affects such as spleen rupture and serious lung problems, along with the more common side effects of severe bone pain and muscle aching.

Mum rolls me into her car and we drive up to the hospital.  Thank goodness it is quiet and I am seen right away in ambulatory care.  This is a pretty easy injection to get, as it is sub-cutaneous.  I did many of these when I was pregnant.  However the short trip is enough to send me over the deep end, so off home we go and back to bed I go.  What a wimp I am becoming.  I sleep for most of the afternoon, then later my friend Lara - super Lara, comes in to give my legs and lower arms a calming massage to help ease the bone pain, which actually hasn't hit yet, but I do very much enjoy her loving touch.  It also makes me very emotional as all loving touch does, so I am a bit of a bundle of tears afterwards.

Later in the evening my sister Marie and her husband Jeff arrive as Jeff is doing the Test of Metal mountain bike race tomorrow morning. This brings over a gaggle of girls (my daughter to see her aunt and uncle and three friends to see the invalid), Rose gets all teary eyed, which leads a few of them to do the same. It is a short visit, including little Ginger, Rose's father's dog. Then I ask everyone to leave, as I need to sleep. Marie and Jeff go out and have a yummy dinner and I have some of Chantal's amazing soup. Fortunately I have only a few bouts with vomiting and nausea, which I manage to catch quickly. The tremendous weakness I feel is the hardest and now the bone pain that is starting is a little worrying. I miss Bob, but Waldo has not left my side since I have been home and that is very comforting.

It is Saturday night, my second evening after the Neulasta and my third evening since receiving chemo. I awaken to a lake of sweat surrounding me. My pretty nightgown and my entire side of the king sized bed are soaked. Mum is sharing the bed with me and wakens the minute I stir. She helps me clean up, gets me one of Bob's long comfy t-shirts and dries off my side of the bed. She wants to change the bedding but I am too tired and just want to go back to sleep. I manage to get a few more hours before it happens again. This time I wake up screaming from a nightmare and once again my bed is soaked. "Poor mum," I think as we go through the process again, this time changing the sheets. I'm going to have to invest in a mattress pad at this rate and sleep on layers of towels. Waldo of course helps in the only way a dog knows how, by creating a distinct cuddle zone between mum and I so none of the yucky chemo junk can soak her side of the bed.

The other weird side affect of the Neulasta is that it seems to take away my ability to effectively manage my limbs and fine motor skills. Walking to the bathroom in the middle of the night is a slow crawl along the wall and any needlework would be out of the question, not that I've ever tried needlework.

I got a lovely message today on Facebook from a friend who was my neighbour from 2004 until 2009. She reminded me of how I've always enjoyed the "spice of life" and lived it to the fullest. My thoughts were always, I'd better enjoy life because what if a bus hits me one day. Well I certainly wasn't expecting a living, ugly transformer style bus that I would have to fight off with all my strength - oh and to make the fight easier for him he decided to compromise my immune system to have an advantage! You don't know whom you're dealing with ASSHOLE!

It's now seven in the morning, time for my first nap of the day. It's going to be a good day today. My dad and his wife are coming up and I think my husband is coming home earlier than expected. Yippee.

I awaken at eleven in a sudden rush to vomit. Like a drunken soldier I make my way to the bathroom and grab onto the toilet bowl for dear life. Mum, hearing my distress, comes into the room to help me. I have to remind her she must put gloves on before touching anything.

How ironic, I think, as I pause between heaves.  The junk they put inside me is so poisonous that mum has to wear gloves if she touches it, so that she doesn't get cancer.  My mind is a jumble of thoughts, sometimes I wish it would stop, I think, as I grip the toilet again and steaming hot liquid tinged slightly red comes shooting out.  When it is all over I am exhausted.  Mum helps me to wash up and I climb back into bed and fall immediately asleep.

I feel like a baby, napping, eating, barfing, napping, eating and barfing some more.

Dad and his wife arrive a few hours later.  It is a very emotional visit.  I feel so awful as I see the sadness in dad's eyes.  I hate causing anyone pain and know that my being sick is causing a lot of people pain.  I am angry with myself but keep it inside and put on a strong front during their visit.  I love my father so much; he is my touchstone, my mentor, and the person I respect more than anyone in the world.  We speak very briefly about my cancer.  I tell them that I have started a blog where they and all my friends can go to learn more about Inflammatory Breast Cancer, as well as to hear how I am doing.  That way I don't have to go through the emotional task of explaining it over and over again.  Most of the visit is spent talking about their trip to France.  I have never been to France and would love to go, so listening to them reminisce is a nice way to get me there in my imagination.

Soon however, I am tired and it is time for me to sleep again.  They say their goodbyes, wish me the best and off they go.  Bob calls just before I go to sleep to let me know he will be home in a few hours, so I let mum know so she can go and catch her ferry. Then I drift off into La La Land with my doggie.

It is Monday morning; I've been lying in bed since about three o'clock waiting for the light to shine in the window so my computer doesn't wake Bob. No such luck, the minute I sit up he's awake. "Sorry honey," I say. "It's just that all through the night I've had this hilarious thought that I've actually been rescued from the Borg by Captain Kirk. They beamed me up to the ship and while I was coming on board Scotty detected a virus within me, so they sent me to sickbay to see Dr. McCoy. Last week he pumped me full of some crazy concoction that he and Data made in the Ten Forward Lounge and today he's getting ready to give me a 'Bone Scan', which for him is very exciting - his nickname is after all 'Bones'." Bob looks at me like I am nuts. "I also have a sneaking suspicion that I might be subjected to his famous probe in places I'd rather not think about." I say.

"Go back to sleep," he says, rolling his eyes.

I cannot sleep though, I am worried about the bone scan I am getting today, and tomorrow I am going to get my hair cut off. I love my hair. It is the best it has ever been; long - past my bra line, and straight – thanks to 'Ice' a Japanese straightening treatment. The colour is a perfect chestnut brown with the occasional red highlight and I have a cut with bangs that offsets my blue eyes beautifully. I will miss my hair. It has become one of my most attractive features and at forty-seven it's good to have a few attractive features still going for you.

As it turns out, I have nothing to worry about with the bone scan. It is the most relaxing test I have had so far. Essentially, they ask you to lie down on a hospital type of bed and relax. The machine does the rest, so I fall asleep. We are back home before supper and after a snack of pineapple and cottage cheese, I go to bed.

Tuesday June nineteenth, wow this chemo is brutal. I had no idea it got worse and worse in the days following the dose. One would think the worst part of chemo is the actual day when you are sitting there "getting the drug". That, my friend, is a breeze compared to what happens in the days that follow. I remember when I went into the chemo ward and saw everyone getting their meds how terrified I was and how surprised I was that they were all sitting there so calmly. Now I know why. The effects take a few days to hit you and they are brutal. An irritating although completely minor side affect is that I am having difficulty using my hands for the most simple of tasks, almost like I have arthritis or some type of motor-neuron disorder. It's frustrating but nothing compared to the other chemotherapy side effects.

I have just come home from the hospital where I was on an IV for fluids, and then they gave me anti-nausea meds and after a few hours sent me home with two more drugs to take. It's insane, I have gone from taking only Advil to now having a drug closet like Keith Richards - I don't know how people keep track of all their meds. After a short nap it's haircut time. Bob drives me to the salon. We take one last photograph of me with my beautiful hair. Meghan, the stylist, takes me to her chair and begins the process of removing my hair that I love so much. She is very kind and gentle and even tolerates it when I have to run to the bathroom halfway in between to get sick. After the cut was done, Meghan gave me a lovely head massage and then styled my hair in a funky little pixie hairdo. My friend Lisa showed up just as we were leaving. A little bird must have told her I was getting my hair cut. She had brought me the most beautiful pair of long glittery earrings. She said that women with short hair need to wear long earrings and she was right. They look so nice and help me feel feminine.

Before I had my first chemo session I was very scared and wondered what it would be like. I went to some websites and read a bit and it sounded awful, but I never thought it could be this bad. I had a dream last night that to me was a good comparison of what it is like going through chemotherapy. Imagine, it's the fifteenth century or some ancient time like that and you're a nice young lad or lady who has been captured by wicked people who are going to use you for their entertainment. They experiment on you, they pump you with drugs, they make you work all night to entertain them and their friends and then during the day you have to clean all their mess. You sleep on a cold brick floor in the pantry and are on some type of drug that they have shoved into you about twenty-three hours of the day. They do this for months on end and then when you are almost dead, a mere shell of the human you were, they slit both your achilles and put you out on the road to freedom. Imagine, months of being abused and completely drug riddled and helpless and now it's your job to heal yourself and get well. That is what my body feels like right now. I want to eat, but food makes me sick, I want to sleep and then I can't get to sleep, my body spends all night boiling out the poison that is inside it, then all day I am sick as a dog. I didn't think it was humanly possible to feel this bad and apparently with each chemo session it gets worse. So I'm in for a hell of a shitty ride over the next year. I know thousands have done this road before me and unfortunately thousands will still have to go down it, but that doesn't make it any better or any easier to accept. Arrgh I think, and sitting here in bed doing nothing is not helping either.

I get up, have a nice hot shower, put on a load of laundry and go to check my email. It has been a few days, since I have checked my email and I bet there is a lot outstanding. The sun is shining through my office window making me wish I could be outside. I can hear Bob outside getting the pool ready for summer fun. I hope I can at least enjoy it a little, I think.

I'm about ten minutes into checking my emails when I realize something is wrong. My heart is racing and my breathing is off. I check the time, eight-twenty. Mary, my assistant, is due at eight-thirty. I'd like to speak to her when she gets here, so I sit a little bit longer at my desk, not reading emails or anything, just sitting. Within minutes I realize this is a bad idea and look outside to see if I can get Bob's attention. He cannot see or hear me. I slowly walk upstairs to my room and lie down. That just makes it worse, now I am really struggling to breathe. I sit upright, grab my phone and send Bob a text. "Please come inside, I need help." There is no answer. Finally Mary comes through the front door. At this point I am in full-blown panic. I slowly make my way down the stairs, and ask her to get Bob. I am terrified. Sitting on the couch I cannot speak or barely breathe. Bob comes running in. "Call an ambulance please," I barely manage to whisper.

Mary brings ice for the back of my neck and I can hear Bob talking to the 911 operator. What is taking so long? Why is the ambulance not here yet? I cannot breathe. I'm going to die here in my own living room. I can't do this, I can't die now, no, and I'm too young. My children, what about my children? All these thoughts are racing through my head as I do my best to try and breathe. Finally I can hear sirens. The firemen were first on the scene and of course who's there but this cute, tall, dark paramedic who I had last seen a few months ago before my diagnosis when he had sold 50/50 tickets at a fundraiser. How embarrassing. That night I, along with seventy or so other crazy screaming women, was all dolled up and pretty with my long hair and jewels. Today I was in my sweats, hair chopped off, barely breathing, looking a complete wreck. Oh how vain we women are, still worried how we look when we're deathly ill. Two ambulance paramedics now arrive. I am relieved but still worried they might be too late. "Oxygen," I say, "I need oxygen". They do an oxygen saturation test and my level is only seventy-five percent, so on goes the oxygen mask. It is making me claustrophobic, but I need it desperately. The first medic cannot get a pulse; this sends me into further panic. One of the medics goes out to get some weird chair contraption to take me from the house to the ambulance while another medic tries again for my pulse. Finally they get it, I don't hear what he says, but I gather it's okay. They strap me to this chair; all the while I am trying to breathe in the oxygen and trying not to die. I look over and see Bob looking at me with fear in his eyes. I cannot speak; I just look at him pleadingly. "Come with me I am thinking."

Once in the ambulance, they strap me down onto the stretcher. I cannot breathe again. "No," I say, "I need to sit upright please." The attendant elevates the head of the stretcher, they close the doors and off we go at full speed, sirens blaring. "Please don't let me die," I beg them over and over again. "Please don't let me die." On the way to the hospital, one of the EMT's speaks to me about chemo. I guess he's taken a few people to the hospital from the affects of chemo. He says it's basically killing me as well as the cancer. Um yeah! I feel that! He says it's going to get worse each time. Really I need to know this right now? He says that if I'm lucky I'll be able to come through it at the other end without cancer. Great! I don't think I want to go back for another chemo treatment EVER if it gets worse or even if it doesn't get worse. If this is what I go through in the days following chemo I don't know if I can do it again. It's bloody terrifying, and what if they hadn't got here fast enough? What if I had passed out and stopped breathing? What will happen next time? I think if I'm going to get chemo, then keep me in the hospital for the seven days following so you can make sure I don't die.

I spend four hours in the hospital. They cannot figure out if I have had an allergic reaction to any of the many medications I am on, or if I had an anxiety attack. My blood work is good, well, as good as someone with cancer and on heavy-duty chemo meds could be. My heart checks out and my breathing is finally back to normal. At two o'clock I am back home all tucked into my comfortable bed and ready to sleep for days. Unfortunately I have to be up by four thirty to go and get my stitches from the biopsy incision removed. Larry, my handsome GP, is very gentle and the stitches are removed without too much pain. He places some suture bandages along the incision, which will eventually come off on their own when the wound is all healed.

After a light dinner of pineapple and cottage cheese again, I am done for the day. However, the events of the last few days have taken their toll on me because a few hours later this is where I find myself, at the beginning of my story, curled up in a ball on my bathroom floor wondering why this is happening to me.

Cancer is bad, but cancer treatment is pure hell.  I just cannot take any more.  I am beyond exhausted and my last thought before I slip into dreamland is "I guess it can't get any worse than this".  Of course little did I know how wrong I was.

## SO THIS IS WHAT HAVING CANCER IS ALL ABOUT

Despite the terrible night's sleep, Friday was a decent day for me. I got some delicious soups delivered by Jenn - yummy! My girlfriend Debbie came to visit. She and my husband made an amazing turkey dinner and I actually sat up with them for a while. Okay I did have a nap mid visit but hell that's what I'm meant to be doing right now. The only challenge I had on Friday was that my brain was still on Crystal Meth. I don't literally mean that I was taking Crystal Meth.

I've never done Crystal Meth or any weird drug but I can only imagine what it must do to your brain. Apparently the Chemo is melting my brain. It feels like the front of my brain is being twisted in a vice and I cannot see properly. My eyes feel all buggy and ache like mad. The back of my brain has this constant hum going on it in and the entire brain is pulsing and throbbing inside my skull. It's like a pump is pumping blood on full thrust up both sides of my neck into my brain and my brain is literally melting and freaking at the same time. Super Gross! It also brings on an all day headache, which is a pain - pun intended. Thank heaven for my girlfriend Lara who came by in a snap and gave me a ten-minute head massage. It felt amazing and also relieved a bit of the pressure.

Saturday was awesome; I got to have my children

overnight for the first time since chemo. My ex and his partner have been so supportive and have been having the children full time to allow me to get better, so to have them yesterday was great, although it did do me in. The first hour was very stressful as Kory had shut down and was not communicating with me. Once we worked through all that, things were fantastic. The kids behaved, mostly and we had a lovely family dinner, the four of us. Bob made a great meal, we sat and talked like we used to over the dinner table, then even had dessert as a family and watched a quirky comedy together. By the end of it all I was shattered, one hundred percent shattered and happy. I went to bed at nine while the rest of the family stayed up and in the middle of the night when I awoke I went into my children's rooms and watched them sleeping for a while. Children are so beautiful when they sleep. They don't argue, they don't talk back or give you looks like you're stupid. They are little angels and boy do I love my little angels. It amazes me that I gave birth to and raised such lovely kids. I am so blessed. They are funny, kind and good hearted. Despite all the stress of parenting, sitting next to them last night all I felt was joy. Pure joy that these were my babies, these beautiful perfect beings that I had created were going to live long and great lives. One day they are going to be adults and explore the world and do incredible things and I will be as proud as I am today. I'm their mother and I adore them. They have helped make me who I am today and for that I am grateful (and have a few more grey hairs). Thanks my monkey.

Keep being great kids.

Today I got the results of my bone scan; here is the email thread between Dr. Sasha and me.

Me: Hey Sasha, do you have the results of my bone scan?

Sasha: Michelle, the bone scan looks very good with the exception of a very subtle area near the left side of your temple. Is this where your headache pain is coming from? The physician reading the bone scan thought that it was likely nothing, but given your headaches a CT of the head may not be a bad idea. I can book this if you are agreeable.

Me: Hi Sasha, that is not where the pain is coming from. I guess let's get a CT Scan of my brain. As long as it doesn't kill/radiate my brain cells. How soon can we do it?

Sasha: Next week easily, and I don't honestly think anything is there...I mean anything bad :-)

So, as you can see, first it all looks good and second I have an Oncologist with a great sense of humour! It helps in times like these.

So today is Sunday and after a good sleep last night I'm ready to have another good day. I am going to try to make it out to watch my son play ball for a while and my sister is coming up for a little visit.


Good morning world, two days without vomiting. I'm feeling great. I have also begun to experience some spiritual enlightenment. My friends could think of a lot of different adjectives to describe me, but I don't think the word "spiritual" would be among them. So what you are about to read may come as a bit of a shock, and it has certainly changed my life over the last few days.

It all started when I heard Anita Moorjani's near death experience. I was absolutely blown away by the powerful message in her story. I thought to myself if she can experience this miracle and go from being on her deathbed from cancer to completely cancer free in less than five weeks, then bloody hell I can do the same, although I'm going to start now. I'm not getting anywhere near my deathbed.

Yesterday I did a Google search for "inspirational cancer healing ideas" and of course who should I find but Louise L. Hay. Years ago when I was going through a tough time, my counselor gave me a book by Louise L. Hay called "You can heal your Life". I was suffering from arthritis in my right hand at the time, and had tried modern medicine through my rheumatologist, but nothing worked. Sharon, my counselor suggested I read the section on arthritis in this book and do the "mantras" or "personal talk" associated with it. I of course put the book on my shelf and ignored it. Then a few weeks later when my hand was all cramped and swollen I thought to myself, what can this hurt. So I did, I tried it, I read the section on arthritis, I read why she thought I had it (apparently I was holding on to something that was not good for me and I needed to let it go), and I looked in the mirror every day for a week and said the sayings to myself. Now I have to tell you that this is awkward. I don't know why but I have no problem talking to myself all day long. Sometimes I even answer myself, but looking into my eyes in the mirror and having a conversation, well that's just odd. I never really got comfortable with it but I have to tell you it worked. Within a week my arthritis was completely gone. That was nine years ago and it has never returned. It made a believer of me, although I never used the book again, other than to look up the occasional ache to figure out what might be causing it.

Finding Louise's name all over these cancer healing sites got me thinking. I can do this, I can use my own inner strength and her guidance and I can heal myself. I just needed something specific to my situation. Then I found it "Cancer, Discovering your Healing Power". I immediately downloaded the audio book and listened to it. I had found the answer. I can do this, not alone, certainly I'm not going to stop going to chemo, however I can heal myself and I have already started.

Within a few hours my body was already feeling better, my breast had stopped aching, which it had been quite badly that day, and my entire mindset was different. I knew that all the support and love I had been getting from my friends and people who I didn't even know cared about me was there for me to draw strength from. I knew that this was not my time, that I still had a lot to do and many years to live on this earth (Yep, Bob I promised I was going to grow old with you and I aim to keep that promise). I felt a strong sense of purpose and I felt I was radiating love all around me. This has stayed with me and continues to strengthen and grow inside me. I am not scared now for my next chemo session. I know that it will provide me with more weapons with which to fight this battle. Actually I don't even think of it as a battle anymore. I am done with cancer. It just hasn't figured that out yet, but my body will eradicate it. Once it has gone, it will never come back because it has no reason to and I won't give it reason. This is experience enough to know I never want it back.

Every morning and every evening now I meditate using the affirmations in Louise's book. I even look myself in the mirror and say the affirmations directly into my eyes. Yes it feels odd but apparently after about a month it won't. In the meantime I am doing it and I feel powerful and I feel good and I am sharing that with everyone around me. I am on my way to being cancer free and all the amazing love and support that my friends and family have given me is working. I am woman - hear me roar! My miracle is happening, just you watch, the doctors will be blown away.

Phew...this is a lot to take in; I can imagine how my Bob must be feeling. I woke up yesterday a completely new woman and he was looking at me wide eyed trying to take it all in. I tell him about meditation and personal power and belief and how I'm healing myself. Wild, the most spiritual I got before this was to ask him for another glass of bubbly to boost my spirits, so this is quite a change.

One of the things I mention is my meditation place. When I meditate, I picture myself on this little beach we went to on our holiday in February, the place called Champagne Bay. I feel such a sense of calm when I think of this place and it is aiding in my healing. I said to Bob yesterday "Honey, when I am healed in a year or two I would like to go back to that little beach. I don't know how we will get there, and right now I'm not going to worry about it, but I want to go there." "We will" he said, "we will find a way and we will go there." It is half way around the world in Vanuatu and it is in my heart as well. I cannot wait for the day I am sitting there again.

I am the luckiest person on this planet; I have the most amazing husband who has been a rock beside me. He has helped with anything I needed and never complained. He is also now supporting me in my spiritual journey of healing and that brings me great joy. I saw my children yesterday morning before school and gave them both great big happy, wild, crazy hugs. I am here guys, I am your mummy and I'm going to be here for a very long time.

This is so amazing. I am no longer "living with cancer," I am healing and everyone around me is helping me to do so. Rejoice with me, become part of my joy and part of my healing process. Watch me grow and become the magnificent beautiful being I was meant to be so I can share with the entire world my experience and help anyone who is experiencing sickness and pain to heal as well. Watch me bring sexy back whether I have cancer or not.  Goodness, I haven't even lost my hair yet.  It has been twelve days since my first chemotherapy session and I haven't even lost a single hair.  Perhaps I cut it for nothing.

Tonight I am having a few friends over for a jewellery party.  I had planned this months ago, before I knew I had breast cancer.  There were days after chemo where I thought to myself, I should call this off, but Clare's pieces are so unique and I really wanted to share them with my friends.  So as each day went by and we got closer to today I monitored my energy levels and by last Friday was sure I could pull this off with no lasting affects.

Clare arrives at five o'clock with huge cases filled with beautiful, sparkly things.  It takes about one and a half hours to set up in the kitchen and dining room.  All the while my little magpie eyes are darting back and forth from bling to bling making my head spin.  I love all of her stuff; of course I couldn't possibly buy it all.  I mean that would be selfish, I should let my friends have some pieces.  Once she sets up I take a few photos to share on Facebook with those who are unable to make it.

Then the craziness begins.  The first to arrive is Anita.  Now I haven't seen Anita in about thirty-one years.  Not since early high school.  It is so great to see her.  She still looks gorgeous - I remember all the guys loving Anita.  I mean, who wouldn't?  She's pretty, has lovely blonde hair, a great smile and she's smart.  Anita brings some lovely flowers to brighten up the room, although with all the bling around I don't think it needs much more brightening up. Then the girls start arriving in droves with food and wine and hugs and smiles, oh and more flowers - thanks Beverly and Barbara.

Imagine if you can, fourteen excited women in a room filled with sparkly jewels and sipping on tasty wine. It is loud and it is a blast. Clare, the designer extraordinaire, and owner of The Magpie's Nest, shows us some of her stunning and functional pieces, such as the necklace extender, the floating bubbles, the fork key chain and many more. It isn't long before each one of us has our heart and our eyes on a little piece of bling we want to call our own.

Around eight o'clock I start to fade, I am already way past overdone but this evening is the most fun I'd had in two weeks, so I don't quite want to go to bed yet. So I sit down on the easy chair and no sooner than I do, I have two of my lovely friends sitting chatting with me. Soon the subject changes to the book '50 Shades of Grey'. Well, you should have heard the energy level rise in the room. I think over eighty percent of us are in the midst of or have read the book. The conversations about sexy, hot, rich, amazing Christian Grey were just plain HOT! Most of us however all wish he were a little older, so we substituted his visual with one of a stunning, sexy, blue-eyed actor who shall remain nameless - maybe he will be in the movie if they ever do a movie. It is Nancy who suggests they make a movie out of the books; I'm not sure how they could do that and allow it in the movie theatre.

Not to mention how would they handle the libidos of the women coming out of the movie theatre. So whom would you want to play Christian Grey? I'm thinking Pierce Brosnan (he'd need to bulk up a bit), Daniel Craig, or perhaps a young Richard Gere hmmmmm...Ohhhh how about George Clooney?

Back on track Michelle, where am I? Oh yes the crazy gaggle of girls going gooey gaga over great gems! So we shop and laugh and eat and drink and then, well I drop! I say my good nights and go up to bed at around nine thirty. Once I get up there I realize my head is pounding beyond belief. As I lay there, Advil trying to do its work, listening to the laughter below I feel at peace. I am in pain, but at peace. It was so great to have such a fun group of women over. The laughter and the joy expressed over Clare's pieces filled those rooms with such positive energy. I was very glad I had not postponed the event. My body may be punishing me for it now, but I had a fabulous time, I felt human again and even though my hair is a little odd, when I'm speaking with people, I can't see it, so I forget it, and I'm once again my old self with long flowing hair and lots to laugh about - although without the wine this time.

I awoke the next day still exhausted, and as I showered I noticed hair coming out in chunks. Oh well, I guess I will not escape the unpleasantness of going bald. On my way to the city today I wrote a little poem to help me accept my baldness.

*Hairdrops keep falling from my head*
*And just like the girl whose tresses were all over her*
*bed*
*My pillow's full of it*
*Those hairdrops keep falling from my head, they*
*keep falling*

*So I just did some talking to my body*
*And I said I thought the way it's doing things is*
*shoddy*
*Sleeping on the job*
*Those hairdrops keep falling from my head, they*
*keep falling*

*But there's one thing I know*
*The loss of my lovely hair won't defeat me*
*It won't be long till baldness steps up to greet me*

*Hairdrops keep falling from my head*
*But that doesn't mean my eyes will soon be turning*
*red*
*Crying's not for me*
*Cause I'm never going to stop the loss by*
*complainin'*
*Because I am free*
*Nothing's worrying me.*

Okay so I'm not bald yet, but little drifts of hair keep
falling past my eyes so I might as well acknowledge the

fact that I'm heading there (no pun intended). So let's talk a little bit about baldness. First I have never been attracted to bald men, no offence to them, I just love a full head of hair on my man. I realize of course that for some men, going bald is not a choice, it's in their genes and unfortunately they just have to live with it, but what I don't understand are those men who are going bald and shave their heads. Or heaven forbid those crazy guys with hair, who think it's attractive to just shave off their nice hair and be naked as a jaybird up top. I mean who told you that was sexy? What are we to run our fingers through? Never mind how it must feel when there's a five o'clock head shadow, gross. I can't imagine how cold their heads get in the winter and why run the risk of sunburn in the summer - nothing super attractive about a blistering red baldhead.

So to all you guys out there who are balding naturally, please keep what is still there, keep it nice and short, it can look sophisticated and even sexy on the right guy and if you are one of those dudes who shaves your entire head for the fun of it, please let it be. You may go bald on your own one day but for now; why not keep your locks while you have them. Women like hair, trust me, those who say they like you bald don't, they just don't want to bruise your egos.

Something that always amazed me is the courageous people who participate in "balding for dollars". I have seen young women with beautiful long hair have it all shaved off to support the cause and I am so awed by them.

What an emotional shock it must be to them to realize in thirty minutes or so it's all gone, the hair they took years to grow is gone. It's not as if one should identify oneself with one's hair, but to lose it all like that, it has to be shocking. It must take great courage and personal fortitude to do go through with it. I applaud you; you're braver than I could be. My going bald is not a matter of choice and given a choice between going bald and adding three extra days a month of feeling shitty through chemo, I'd choose feeling shitty. It's not just vanity speaking; ever since I have cut my hair my head has been cold and I bet it's contributing to my twenty-four hour headache. Oh well suck it up chicky pooh. As my girlfriend Trish would say "Put your Big Girl Panties on" and deal with it, and as Telly Savalas would say "We're all born bald, baby."

It has been two weeks since my first chemotherapy session and I'm starting to feel human again. Prior to chemo, I was able to go for long dog walks or ride with my dog for at least five kilometers a day. Riding, as with driving a vehicle is impossible for me right now because the chemotherapy has affected my sense of balance and my vision. However I am able to walk. Walking though has taken on a whole new meaning and requires all my gumption to get me doing it. I start the day after chemo, Bob has to go with me and typically the most I can manage without passing out or becoming severely short of breath is a snail's pace walk around the block.

I push myself to do this every day, not just for the health reasons, but also for my sanity. I have to keep on living; I cannot succumb to depression and atrophy in my bed. Cancer requires a strong mind and a strong body to beat it, and I intend to kill this sucker. Now that it is two weeks past the first chemo I have managed to get my walks to around four blocks, moving incredibly slowly, but I'm getting better. This morning I had the shock of my life when I looked in the mirror and noticed my previously muscular thighs were skinny and flabby. They looked exactly like my mother's thighs. Now for a seventy-four year old, my mother has great gams, but they look a little odd on a forty-seven year old, especially one who has been fit all her life. I have to suck it up a little as I realize my energy levels over the next eight months of chemotherapy will have a huge impact on my fitness but I vow to continue doing what little I can to keep some muscle mass so when I get better I will bring it all back.

Tonight my friends Michele and Debbie are coming over for wine in the Oasis. Yes, I have an Oasis now. Over the past month Bob has worked double time to complete the back yard project that we started last year. We were challenged by the budget and how we could afford to complete a three-year plan in this year, so I sat down with him and had a frank conversation. I said that we needed to up the timeline on this project for two reasons. My first concern was when I died I wanted to make sure it was finished because if Bob decided to sell the house, it would make it a lot easier to sell with a finished back yard. This reasoning angered him and he didn't want to hear it. He was far more convinced by the second reason, which was that I needed a nice, quiet place to recover in over the summer. A place where I could sit in the shade and watch the children frolic in the pool, even if I could not join them, at least I wouldn't be closed away in my bedroom upstairs.

So Bob agreed and slaved away outside for hours and now I have a lovely Tiki Bar, large deck area with covered gazebo section that has couches and chairs for friends to comfortably sit in. The swimming pool is in and almost heated to my desired twenty-eight Celsius and he is finishing off the barbecue and hot-tub area. It looks lovely. The Tiki Bar has a real thatched roof and a beer fridge in the back. I took the ugly old planters from the garden, cleaned them up and they now sit at the back of the large deck area with Hostas and solar lights in them. I designed the deck so that it would go around the lovely lush shrub on the left side, allowing some greenery to be a part of it and also providing a cooling effect. We have two small willows on either side of the deck area, which have also been incorporated into the space, and the rear fence, instead of being a full fence is slatted to allow the green from the large fir hedge to show through. All in all it is paradise, which is why I named it the Oasis.

So here we are, Debbie, Michele and I sipping champagne under the shade of the gazebo in the Oasis. Michele had just arrived back a few days ago from her trip to Europe and I was so happy to be spending time with her again. Although she was only gone three weeks, so much had happened during that time and prior to my getting sick, we got together at least twice a week to walk the dogs or share a bottle of wine, it was precious time that I had missed terribly. As we three chat as only women can, the subject of Nora Ephron comes up. Nora had died three days ago at the age of seventy-one. She was an amazing women and an inspiration to us all, showing everyone what is possible. Michele reminds us of one of Nora's powerful quotes, "Oh, how I regret not having worn a bikini for the entire year I was twenty-six. If anyone young is reading this, go, right this minute, put on a bikini, and don't take it off until you're thirty-four."

How true this quote is. The three of us chatting are now in our late forties and most people would say that all three of us are pretty, vivacious, attractive women, and on some days we may even agree with them. However, none of the three of us saw what a great thing we had when we were younger. What's with that? Was it to protect the men out there? I mean imagine what forces we women would have been if we'd had the confidence we have now, at the age of sixteen, twenty-one, and twenty-five etc.

This reminded me of a conversation I'd had with my mother a few days earlier. We were talking about when women "come into their own" and start to truly love themselves and believe in themselves. My mother said for her it didn't happen until she was in her late fifties. For me it was in my late thirties. I can only hope that the pattern continues and that the daughters of today are getting that confidence in their teens. It saddens me to see beautiful young girls like my daughter and her friends so worried about their looks and their weight. Girls, don't you see how stunningly beautiful you all are? No matter what you look like you were made to be exactly who you are - you are beautiful and magnificent. You don't need make up or diets or clothes to bring that out. You need confidence and love and a strong sense of self worth. Take it from someone who has been there and is now looking back. If you can realize now how special and unique you are, then you have such power. No one can put you down; no one can make you feel bad about yourself because you know beyond a shadow of a doubt that you are great. Embrace this now, and as you mature you will witness the many ways in which your body matures along with you. When we are young we are fresh and alive, new spirits in this world. As we grow older each one's persona becomes defined. The edges are clearer, the beauty radiates more and the combination of our confident inner self and our blossoming outer self is mind blowing. Ask any man. There is nothing sexier than a strong, beautiful confident woman. Embrace that, become that and never let it go. There is nothing sadder than someone reaching old age and never having really lived the life they were meant to live with passion and integrity.

So grab some balls girls, listen to your mother and friends when they say you're beautiful and kind and wonderful. Be that person. Live a big large life. Make it yours and make it fun. As one of my favourite sayings goes (I changed it and put the "bubbly" in):

"Life should not be a journey to the grave with the intention of arriving safely in an attractive and well preserved body, but rather to skid in sideways - glass of bubbly in one hand - chocolate in the other - body thoroughly used up, totally worn out and screaming 'WOO HOO, What a Ride".

Now get your butts out there girls and go live it.

Yes, we three certainly had a fun night in the Oasis. I called it a night at around nine and left the two of them out there to finish the champagne and enjoy the lovely summer evening. As I got into bed I checked my iPhone for new emails. There was a message from my oncologist. The CT Scan I had done on my head following the bone scan had come in. The results were fine. I have my own private island. Yes, you heard that correctly. I have what is called a 'Brain Island' in my skull bone. "It's nothing to worry about," noted my oncologist, "be grateful we also found a brain in there." So this is good now, no cancer in the rest of my body, just the pesky junk in my breast and lymph nodes to get rid of.

The rest of the weekend was relatively quiet. Everyday I felt a little bit better, I managed a morning walk with Waldo, followed by a long nap, and then in the afternoon I sat in the Oasis reading. I had been sent so many cancer books it was overwhelming, books on what to eat, what not to eat, books about alternative medicine, books telling you chemo killed you, it was endless. I felt a duty at least to look at them and make my own decisions. My brother Sean had kindly given me his juicer, so for now Bob was making me all kinds of health concoctions. They all tasted like the garden to me, but according to all research, they were very good for me, and certainly couldn't do me any harm.

The weather was very warm for early July, especially in our back yard, where the wind barely passed through. This is a terrific thing for swimming and hanging out on deck chairs in the sun, but not so great for a chemo patient who is going through menopause. Yes, chemo kicks you through menopause. The hot flashes started almost immediately and they are wicked. One minute I am fine, the next minute I have to rip my clothes off instantly. Sometimes I cannot get them off fast enough and I feel as if I'm going to explode. So when one of these flashes hits me while I am sitting outside I run upstairs to my air-conditioned bedroom and strip down. There I lie, panting, waiting for my body temperature to drop. Soon I am cold enough to require a light sheet on me, and curl up and fall asleep. I awaken a few hours later in a puddle of sweat, even though the air conditioner is on high. Oh the joys of chemotherapy and menopause. As my body is slowly pushing the poison out through the sweats and its natural filtration system, I start to feel a little more normal. Following that is a feeling of uselessness. I feel that I should be doing more than resting all day. Surely I could help with something around the house. So one evening after a particularly hot day and many bodies swimming in the pool I decide to scoop out the leaves and junk that has found its way into the pool during the day. What a joke that was. I picked up the pool skimmer, did about three skims, and was feeling very proud of myself when I realized like a gas tank, my gauge had just gone from half full to completely empty in less than two minutes. I rather ashamedly put the skimmer down and slink back inside, get a glass of cold water and rest on the couch. So much for my 'get up and go'.

## GOING BALD, AMONGST OTHER THINGS

People who know me see me as a woman who charges through life and tackles things head on. So this morning when I showered and chunks of my spunky short hair were falling off into my hands and down the drain I thought to heck with this. The hair will be gone in a week anyway, why mess up my drains, carpets and bed with two-inch chunks of hair. So I called Meghan and asked if she could shave my head for me. I didn't want it completely bald, but about one eight of an inch in length so that the "falling out process" didn't look so odd and make such a mess.

So I did it! No tears this time. All smiles as I went in and she shaved away. I'm not sure what I was expecting, however the end result was still a little shocking for me. I haven't touched it yet, that just seems a little alien still, but I'm sporting the new look proudly. I think I'm going to handle the "bald" thing better than expected, not that I'm going to like it but I will make the best of it.

Originally I had told my daughter that when I was bald I was going to get something tattooed on the back of my head. Not having any previous tattoos I really had no idea what I was talking about. The thought was good, but really? What am I going to put at the back of my head? Some saying? Some odd little character? I can't think of anything that resonates with me, and what if it stops my hair from growing back in properly? I believe that if we are going to get a tattoo it needs to be meaningful because we have it for the rest of our lives. Granted a tattoo on the back of my head will never be "in my face" reminding me of Bubba or some crazy serpent and flower combination that I thought meant something at the time. However I still don't see the point in it.

As a mother raising children in a time where young girls and boys think it's sexy to have colourful tattoos all over their bodies I am challenged with helping guide my children towards respecting and not defacing the bodies that they have. I am not against tattoos if they are chosen with great care, are small and are not visible unless one is in ones birthday suit. The trouble is, what sixteen, eighteen or twenty-one year old can make a decision on a tattoo that will be meaningful to them all their lives. Remember when you were young and you thought a rose with a dagger through it and your girlfriends name written over it was cool. Or how about the barbed wire around your wrists and ankles - not so cool now. When Bob and I were on our cruise this past February we saw what I thought was the funniest tattoo ever. It was across the stomach of a forty something man. It was obviously a tattoo from over ten years ago when he had a six-pack. Even then it would have been, well, arrogant. Now it was just hilarious. Written in big letters across his extremely large beer belly were the words "Gods Gift to Women". Yes. I'm serious. That is what he had written very clearly across his belly. The funny thing was, this man, definitely past his prime, was still acting like he was "Gods Gift to Women". Perhaps it was all the rum drinks or the case of beer that he had drunk on the pool deck that day, but he was parading around and bossing his women around like he owned the place. I guess I should thank him for providing me and the other stunned people by the pool with something to laugh at.

That being said, I heard a great tattoo idea the other day and actually went online to check it out. Apparently there is a famous tattoo artist in Seattle who specializes in tattooing to cover scars. In particular she works with women who have had mastectomies and wish to cover the scars with something beautiful. I have to admit the work I saw was Art. One of the women had chosen a tattoo that took four years to complete. It was a dragon of sorts that went all the way from her stomach up around both breasts and along the scars to her shoulders. It was beautiful. Too big for me and there is no way I would have the patience to take four years to see the end result. If I were to do this I would choose perhaps some simple ivy or chain or something that went along the length of the scars, and maybe one day I will consider it. For now, having not got to the surgery part yet, my thoughts are that the scars should heal quite well and a little scar might be better than a big tattoo. Who knows? Only time will tell.

Tonight I spoke to Bob about the possibility of going on a holiday with the children. I am not sure how much longer I am destined to be on this planet and I would like to do a family holiday with them before I get too sick to be able to. We discussed a Mexican cruise out of Los Angeles, a trip to Disneyland or a possibly even a trip to Las Vegas. The key points for me were, not too long a flight and a place where the children would be safe and I could relax. I love cruising and this was the preferred destination for me, but for a family of five it was too costly. We wanted to bring Bob's daughter Anna, which would mean booking two cabins instead of one, and that doubled the price. Disneyland, a place that I love to go to would be good. We might be able to get a hotel that would allow five of us to share the room, and everyone would enjoy the rides. Then Bob reminded me of how much I like to do the rides and how I won't be able to and how exhausting walking around a theme park all day will be for me. I guess that ruled that out.

The last option was Las Vegas. I had been to Vegas once before on a business trip. We stayed in the Bellagio, a hotel that I loved, but I had no time for Vegas itself. I don't gamble and just found the entire experience a waste of time and money. Bob has been to Vegas a lot and said the reason I didn't like it was because it was a work trip and it was in January and the weather was cold. He has suggested a few times over the years that we go to Vegas, but I have always turned him down. My children really wanted to go to Vegas. I think it was all because of the television show Pawn Stars. They were convinced this was Vegas and it was fun, and they have been asking to go for a while. So I started looking at prices. Again we needed two rooms, as no rooms would allow a family of three adults and two children.  The Bellagio was out of the question and I wasn't willing to stay in an off the strip dump, so we searched for a while until I found The Tropicana.  They had newly renovated, had a huge pool and looked nice and clean.  The price including airfare was very good, and I had been led to believe by Bob that Vegas was cheap.  "This may be an option," I think.  I just need some time to think about it.

It is July fifth already and time for my second round of chemotherapy.  I'm a little nervous, but other than that fine.  What I don't know is how amazing the human body is at erasing bad memories for us.  On the way in I do some meditation with an Abraham/Hicks meditation CD I had downloaded onto my iPhone.  We pick up Timbits to give to the nursing staff and then I weigh in and find myself a bed against the wall.

Sasha comes to see me and I ask him if he thinks I will be able to do a holiday with my family.  He suggests it as a good thing to do, however to time it for a week before a chemo dose, because that is when I am feeling my strongest.  It is nice to get his approval.  Now we just need to make our decision.

My second dose of Tiger's Blood (that is what I call the Adriamycin because it is bright red) was administered quite easily today.  Eat your heart out Charlie Sheen!  I have the real stuff. I lay there while the "Healing Potion" as I am now calling it, courses through my veins and goes to find and annihilate the cancer cells.  It isn't long before I fall asleep and I continue to sleep all the way home in the car.

Apparently Michele came to visit me after I was home and spent some time sitting in the chair at my bedside. I do not remember a thing. Once again, the first twenty or so hours are a complete blur. What follows is another week of pure hell. Yes, I had forgotten how horrible chemotherapy is. To be honest, I have fallen into a pit of despair. I wonder what the use is of all of this. From what I am researching, chemo, radiation and surgery is no cure, it's only making things worse for me and is no guarantee that the cancer won't come back. So why am I bothering to do it at all? I feel it is taking away what little life I have left and making it a hellhole.

I want my old life back. I hate this cancer. Why did it have to happen? Why can't I just go back to normal? I just want to be normal. I want to go out with my friends, drive my car, walk my dog, play with my kids, cuddle my kids, go out for dinner with my husband, go on a vacation, do normal things. What I would give for NORMAL. This life totally sucks and I'm only on chemo number two of seventeen, what is the damn point. A whole year and a half taken from my life. A whole year and a half where my kids won't have a functional mum and for what? So I can spend the next two years recovering from the ravages of chemotherapy and then maybe live one more year before it all comes crashing back?

I will never be the same. Life for me is not life anymore. I feel like a robot, just ticking along doing what I'm supposed to be doing, taking the chemo and all the crap and doing what should be done because that's what the doctors say. I don't want this. There must be a better way. I am not a proper wife or mother anymore and that is horrible. I have all these people whose lives have now changed because of me. I hate that. This is a horrible burden on everyone and for that I am sorry.

It takes me six days of vomiting, forcing myself to get out of bed and walk around the block, sleeping away the days and wishing I would die to bring me out of this second round of drug induced hell. I awaken feeling a little better on Wednesday morning; I think I have managed to find my way back up out of this pit and into some sense of normalcy again. That's not to say I have tons of energy and feel like a human being again, more that I've passed through this particular phase of chemo side affects and the associated depression that goes along with it. I have certainly learned a few things from it.

First, I need to find some form of counseling so I can manage the depths of my despair a little better and understand that what I am going through is a normal part of what anyone who is faced with a cancer diagnosis goes through. I have heard it said that many cancer patients suffer from PTSD at some point in time after getting the "diagnosis or label", and that this depression can last months or years. So when seen in that perspective my little dip down into hell isn't that bad. I know that I'll have many more of them over the next year or so and the most important thing for me is to make sure that I can find my way out of them. I hate seeing myself sitting on the bathroom floor crying so hard my body aches, but I also know that this is a good way for me to "get out" the icky feelings inside rather than to let them bottle up and fester. This leads me to the second thing that I have learned from this little experience.

Some people feel uncomfortable with my sharing my desperation. It seems that I am viewed as a fighter and a strong person who doesn't have a weak side. Well, I guess I do have a softer side, and every once in a while it will come to the surface. Please understand that talking about this is very therapeutic for me. It is a way for me to vent my feelings and try to sort out how I'm going to continue to fight this disease. I know people don't want to acknowledge that I am going to die, but I need to. I need to discuss it out in the open, to understand it and make it real so I am not afraid of it. When I am really down in the dumps do not despair, I will find my way out. I'm just going through the process of coming to an acceptance of my situation and struggling to find a balance and a new normal.

Now on to other things. Last night, my husband, in all his brilliance, came up with the perfect analogy for my situation. Imagine if you will that you have been arrested, charged and convicted of a crime that you did not commit. Suddenly out of nowhere the police show up at your door, take you away, sit you in a cold sterile room and tell you that you are guilty of some heinous crime and that the judge has already decided your fate. You have no choice in the matter. Your fate is a fifteen-month prison sentence during which time you will be subject to all measures of nastiness and you just have to suck it up. Afterwards if you are a really good prisoner, you just may be allowed to continue life with a tracker around your ankle that could go off at any time and send you back, or if you haven't responded well, then to heck with you, you can just die with the others. Okay so I have added a bit to his analogy here, but I think you get the point. To be in that situation, so completely powerless and at the mercy of "others" (in my case doctors) is extremely difficult to manage. Especially for a Type A control freak like me. So being a typical Type A take-control kind of girl, I am trying to find my way to control this even if it's only on the edges. I have found an excellent naturopath (referred to me by my GP), who specializes in treating patients who are going through Cancer and more specifically chemotherapy. With his advice I will come up with a nutritional and alternative treatment plan that will go hand in hand with the chemo. Unfortunately his services are not recognized by the "establishment" so are not covered by BC Medical or my extended health plan, but I do believe they will help me get through the poisoning sessions over the next year and a half. It is also my understanding that some of the changes I will be making by working with him will help to keep the big bad demon away in the future, and I'm all for that.

The other areas that I am now focused on (because I can control them) are my spiritual and general physical health. I have always been obsessed with my weight. I know its nuts and it feels so shallow now but it was a big thing for me. Ever since I've been a teenager I've been vigilant about weighing myself daily. I mean it didn't help that I was endearingly called "little fats fats", "little sausage" and other such well-meaning terms. You see I was never really fat as a child, but I had a chubby little face, which people found cute and so the nicknames were meant lovingly, but I think they left an impression on me. As a result I've always exercised and yes maybe once or twice dieted, but typically I preferred the exercise. The great thing about this is that even at my age, I can honestly say that up until a month ago, I still had a good body, firm and strong. Then chemo hit. I do mean chemo, not cancer, because the cancer didn't really make me sick. I was certainly tired during the months of March, April and May, however I assumed it was due to my travels and my work, not an illness. However once I started getting chemotherapy, even walking around the block has been a challenge. My once muscular legs are now flappy little beanpoles and it's gross. So, that is something I can slowly control and bring back. I am doing twenty minutes of Yoga (on the mornings I don't feel like barfing) and am slowly adding in a little bit of resistance training. The hope is that I can build back a little of what I have lost and maintain some strength for the fight. I do believe if I am physically stronger then it will be easier on me. As to the spiritual health, I'm continuing with my daily Louise Hay and have added Abraham/Ester Hicks meditations into the fray. I am also looking for a retreat of sorts where I can rest and heal mentally.

I'm back on the upside and managing to take things day by day. I spend a lot of time sitting in our backyard Oasis that Bob has spent so many hours building. It is peaceful and quiet (mostly) and gives me a chance just to relax, which I realize now I have never really done before. Even on holidays I am so Type A that I schedule everything. When we went to Disney World in 2007 I even had every park mapped out and which rides we were going to do in what sequence programmed into my blackberry (before I got an iPhone), all of course done to maximize our enjoyment and minimize our waiting in line ups, but wow, how anal, how controlled. So, this new me is going to be the Chillax Girl. The Mañana Girl! Well, I will try at least.

Today is another beautiful day in Sea to Sky country so I decide to venture outside for a short bike ride rather than a short walk with my dog. Since the chemo my vision has gone crazy making me unsafe to drive a car, so I am not sure how riding a bike will go.

Luckily it went well, very slowly without any major falls. I was weaving all over the road but there were no cars coming, so it was okay. We only went about four blocks, just enough to give the dog a run (he and Bob ran ahead super fast and waited for me to catch up) and to tire me out for the day. I think it's going to take a few months before I'm back up to any distance on my bike.

One little ride and I'm out like a light on the steps with my Doggie. The breeze is nice so this is the best place for us to catch a few zzzz's. After only about three and a half hours of sleep last night I needed a nap. I decided last night to not take my sleeping pill (I only want to take them when I'm going through the worst of the chemo side effects), so needless to say I was up until two in the morning putzing around the house with a pounding headache. When I finally did fall asleep I had the most vicious nightmares - thanks to the Low Dose Naltrexone, which funnily enough I forgot to take yesterday. I got the nightmares regardless, and they are brutal, recently they have been all about the crushing of skulls and torture and evil stuff. Sometimes my nightmares (even prior to chemo) have been so terrifying I have woken Bob up with my screams. Even though they are more brutal, I don't seem to be waking up yelling. I just wake up saying "what the hell was that, I just crushed someone's head in with a pan." Yikes!

I am fully bald now and it feels quite good. I am lucky, my head is well shaped, and so being bald is actually not too bad. It helps me to keep cool during the hot summer nights but when I am out I wear a scarf or hat to cover the white head.   My children are very embarrassed about it, so I try to respect their feelings by never surprising one of their friends with my bald head.

Today is my daughter's birthday. I cannot believe Rose is now eleven. I remember when she was born. She was born on a Friday the thirteenth, three weeks early.

What a lovely baby she was. She cuddled from the very beginning, always wanting to be close to me and she is still like that. She is very exhausting and never stops for a second but she is kind and loving and I adore her. It saddens me to think that I may not be around to see her become a teenager, have boyfriends, hold her when she cries over her first broken heart and rejoice with her when she gets accepted into the university she chooses. I want so badly to be here for all those things. It will take a miracle.

This morning, Bob and I leave town relatively early for an appointment with a Naturopath in Kerrisdale. It is a beautiful drive down, perfect weather, no traffic to speak of (until we hit the city of course), and great conversation. Since I am a little early we stop in to my office to check mail and say hello. It is nice to see everyone who is there - I guess only I have changed, for the rest of the world nothing is new.

I spend one hour and forty-five minutes with Dr. Lemon (not his real name), and it is well worth every second of my time. Let me explain, Dr. Lemon is a Naturopathic Oncologist. His specialty is working with cancer patients and he works a lot in tandem with my particular Oncologist at the Hospital. My reason for wanting to see Dr. Lemon is to find some ways to manage the ravages that chemo has on the body and to try to keep my body strong so it can survive all these chemo sessions.

His expertise blows me away. We discuss everything from the chemo doses and other medications I am on, to the exercise I do or don't do daily, the relaxation I do or don't do daily and any stressors that may be in my life other than the cancer situation. With that information, and having a full knowledge of my medical history, Dr. Lemon and I put together a plan to provide me with everything I need to keep strong and recover. It's pretty intense, and involves reducing a few of the drugs I am currently on (such as the MASSIVE steroid drug I didn't even know I was having to take), and adding in about eight other supplements as well as adding Cabbage (which I love) into my current juicing routine. Dr. Lemon mentions that the fact that I am already having one juice from the juicer a day is one of the best things I could be doing for my body. We are upping it to two juices now - thanks Sean.

So it turns out the heart issues I was having on day three through five after each chemo session are a result of the crazy steroid I had to take, not the chemo drugs. Also the steroid is affecting my ability to sleep. So with dropping that dosage down and adding in Glutamine Power, Vitamin D, Fish Oil (already taking), Curcumin, Low Dose Naltrexone (already taking), Melatonin, Tryptophan and possibly IV Vitamin C twice a week, I should feel like a champion by the time my next chemotherapy session is due. I feel so empowered. I am doing something good for my body that will give me strength to manage the crash after each chemo session.  I am woman - hear me ROAR!

I also asked Dr. Lemon his opinion on the Port-a-

Cath that the Hospital wants to install in my chest for administering the chemo sessions. He said if he or anyone in his family got cancer he would get it installed right away, so I have booked my appointment for that in the first week of August. I left the meeting feeling that my care was in good hands from both these fine professionals (Sasha and Dr. Lemon), and that I am now finally comfortable trusting completely in them to do the right thing for me. I of course am still responsible for my mental and physical health, which I'm taking very seriously too.

After the doctors appointment, we rush over to West Vancouver as I am meeting Rose and three of her friends at Refine Express Spa. Refine Express is a fabulous, relaxing place to go for anything from manicures to bodywork and facials. Instead of a party, Rose wanted a spa session here with her girlfriends and when I got there they were all set up with their feet and hands soaking and ready for their afternoon. I got a couple of great surprises at the Salon. First my girlfriend Rikke who I hadn't seen in ages had found out we were going to be there so she stopped in to join the adults for lunch. Second, my friend Kathie had heard I was going to be there and had taken some time to pick up some lovely colourful scarves, so there she was all smiles and bling with this lovely gift and hugs.

After some chitchat, Jenn, who had driven Rose and her friends in to the salon, Rikke and I go to The Fish House for lunch. It is so nice and relaxing although I do notice I'm not my old self. I normally enjoy the warmth from the sun, however two minutes of sitting in it and I feel like I am going to hurl, so we finally get seated under an umbrella. What a relief. The other difference is that normally on a lovely, sunny day like this, sitting on a patio, not having to drive, I would have a few glasses of crisp white wine. No such luck these days. A half a glass mixed liberally with soda and I'm done. Such a shame, really, on the other hand, wine is fattening, so there is a benefit here too.

We have a leisurely lunch and lots of terrific conversation and before we know it, it is time to go back and get the girls home. After some big goodbye hugs for Rikke, we load four over excited little girls into the car. By this point I am so tired I think I'll drop, so I try to relax on the way home. Hard to do when the girls are singing beautifully at the top of their lungs right behind you. However we make it and I even make a dramatic suggestion on the way home. "Hey girls, how would you like to come over for a swim in the pool followed by pizza and cake?" I mean who wouldn't jump at that? The day is warm, the pool is thirty-two degrees Celsius and the party is still on. I rest on the couch (after of course cleaning the kitchen - anal), while two adults sit outside sipping on wine and beer and watch the kids having a blast. Even Kory joins in. He is in the pool as long as all the girls (probably two hours), which is a first for him. It makes me so happy to hear the sounds of children's giggles and enjoyment coming from the back. When I originally designed our backyard I had two thoughts in mind. I wanted to create an "Oasis" where we can have relaxation or adult parties in the evenings and also a place where my kids will come, with their friends to swim in the pool, have cold pop at the Tiki Bar and pretty soon sit by the fire pit or in the hot tub. So today hearing the joy coming from the back is like hearing part of my dream come true. It brings a huge smile to my face. I only wish I could be in the pool with them.

At around seven-thirty it is time for things to wrap up and many hours past when I should have shut things down. So the kids get all dressed and I clean up. Just as they are leaving the third amazing thing happens in my day. My friend Lisa had seen my Facebook post from a few days ago asking if anyone knew where I could buy nice cotton bandannas or scarves in town, or if anyone had any they didn't use anymore. So she went into a very expensive shop in Yaletown yesterday to see if they had any, and lo and behold she found a beautiful one. It's like a bandanna or scarf, but it's already sewn to fit and it's silk and has long ties that you can do many things with. When Lisa asked the sales clerk how much, she was told one hundred and sixty-five dollars. It is a little over the budget for a scarf, lovely that it may be. Anyway, the sales lady (who by the way didn't own the store), went to the back, wrapped it in a box, came back out and said to Lisa, you know what, I've had some good things done for me this week, so I'd like to "pay it forward" and purchase this scarf for your friend. Lisa was blown away, as am I. So today Lisa arrived with said scarf. I have to tell you it's magical. It fits easily, I don't have to tie it because it's sewn the right way and it's comfortable and you can make it shaped in different ways. Lisa and I both think our mutual friend Lorraine would be able to make couple just like it in silk or soft cotton with prints to match my outfits. I will have to go and thank the amazing salesperson when I am next in town.

So all in all, I had a spectacularly large day, full of joy, new insights, love, love and more love from my dear friends and now I am at peace, sitting in bed with my doggie waiting for my husband to come home. What more could a woman ask.

Good night world. Some days you just rock.

## RIDING THE CHEMOTHERAPY ROLLERCOASTER

Going through chemotherapy has turned my world upside down. I am incapable of doing even the simplest of tasks, and my brain has turned to complete mush. All I am good for these days is sleeping, eating and sitting for hours staring into space. Of course, as I approach the next chemo session I am becoming restless. My body is still unable to do much physically so I have to find ways to keep my mind busy. Today I spent time researching Cancer Treatments. Now I feel like a chicken with my head cut off. The number of alternative treatments and opinions out there is just mind-boggling. One needs a PhD in Quackology to figure out which ones are real and which are not.

There are clinics in Mexico, Germany, Hungary, USA, you name it. They range in cost from fifteen thousand dollars plus the cost of accommodation in local hotels to one hundred thousand dollars and up. They offer everything from chelation therapy to coffee enemas. Yes you read that correctly "coffee enemas". Some reports say that chemo will kill you and to stay away from it and go on their program only. Some clinics advocate a combination of traditional (chemo, radiation and surgery) and alternative treatments. Some quote survival rates of eighty percent versus twenty-five to thirty percent with traditional. With all this information out there it's no wonder patients struggle to figure out what to do. A lot of people will automatically accept their doctor's recommendation for traditional treatment and never look further. For those who do decide to explore alternative methods, I can only hope you are educated, intelligent and have a strong sense of self, otherwise you could be suckered into spending all kinds of money on a treatment plan that piques your interest and may not necessarily work for you.

One of the things I like about most of the alternative treatment options is that they are individualized. With traditional treatment it is a one size fits all approach. They do not do any testing such as Oncotype DX (a genomic test that analyzes the activity of a group of genes that can affect how a cancer is likely to behave and respond to treatment), Biofocus (a test that offers a chemo sensitivity test that allows you to know which chemotherapeutic agents will work most effectively against your particular cancer cells) or the Ex-Vivo Analysis—Programmed Cell Death (EVA-PCD) test (a platform that creates a functional profile of your cancer's sensitivity and resistance to various drugs and combinations.) With this profile, your oncologist is equipped with the most accurate information to treat your cancer and to see if the treatment they are recommending is the correct one for you. Cancer is a profitable business for hospitals, doctors and drug companies. The drug companies push the doctors to prescribe their drugs, the hospitals don't want additional tests that may mean additional costs, and the doctors are looking for the safest (for them) and easiest way to provide treatment. So hence, the blanket approach is used unless the patient doesn't do well, in which case the doctors will consider other "traditional, big pharma" treatments. Now I'm not saying these don't work, they just don't (according to statistics) seem to work very well. It is my belief that a combination of traditional and alternative is the way to go. Especially for me because the aggressive nature of my cancer does not afford me the time it may take for gentler more alternative treatments to work.

With this in mind, I have found an alternative treatment that makes sense to me, has a proven track record and is the least expensive of the possible effective options available. So, I am going to be asking for my Oncologists blessing to proceed with Intravenous Vitamin C treatment. If he approves it then, twice a week I will be receiving the treatment at a cost of one hundred and thirty to one hundred and fifty dollars per session for the first six months, then weekly for the following six months and monthly thereafter. It is a small price to pay if it can help heal the cancer and keep it away. The only concern I have going in to it is my veins. As it is, I am having surgery on August 7th to install a Port-a-Cath in my chest. This will help with the problem the nurses have in finding my veins and to stop my veins from getting damaged during chemo. With the IVC protocol, they don't do that, they have to find a vein every time, and for me that is a task and a half.

One other thing I decide today is that I need to remove myself from the IBC support page on Facebook.

I'm not saying it is bad, but it isn't for me. I find it very depressing to get posts on a daily basis that so and so passed away last night, and so and so passed away yesterday and on and on. I already know the statistics on IBC are not great, but I believe that I have an advantage because I am young, fit, strong and have a positive no-lose attitude. Hearing all this sad news on a daily basis is not good for my psyche. So bye bye negative, hello positive. I have five days until my next chemo session and I'm going to spend them getting strong and preparing both mentally and physically for the onslaught. Tomorrow I am going to a healing session with horses - it should be interesting. I am also doing a presentation in my office about the insane costs of having cancer and the role Critical Illness Insurance has in providing peace of mind to the patient, allowing them to focus on recovery, not money. If there is one lesson I have learned through all of this, it is the value of having proper insurance coverage.

I didn't ask to be a poster child for Critical Illness Insurance, but here I am, I think as I look up into the blue sky.  Today is a beautiful day, the Tantalus range looks glorious with the sun lighting the remaining snow on its peaks. Time to get off my butt and take Waldo for a walk. Having cancer does not give me an excuse to not enjoy living, especially on days like this.


It's Monday July twenty-third.  Today is the day I give a presentation at work on Critical Illness and then afterwards I am going to the healing retreat. Getting up early on a Monday morning reminds me of my working days. I miss those days, I miss having a purpose.

After a quick shower and coffee I am on my way to the city. Once again we have been blessed with a beautiful summer day. Blasting my music as I drive down the Sea to Sky makes me feel almost normal, almost as if I don't have cancer. Correction, I think to myself, don't have a 'terminal' cancer. That is how IBC is described, as terminal, eighteen-month average survival rate, blah, blah, blah. However, I'm different, I have to believe that. I simply cannot allow myself to focus on my mortality, not yet, not now. So I smile, wipe away the tears and enjoy the drive, turning the music a little louder as I do, only happy thoughts today. I must not break down during this presentation.

I arrive at the branch office in record time and the parking attendant smiles broadly as I drive into the parkade. It has been a while since we have seen each other, but she remembers me. When I get upstairs the meeting room is full, it is standing room only. Seeing my colleagues for the first time since my diagnosis is difficult. I can see the sadness in their eyes, the pity. In a way it frustrates me, but I realize most of them do not understand, and I hope they will never have to understand.

The presentation went well and afterwards there were lots of hugs and well wishes. Richenda had baked me some delicious cookies and I also got a box of truffles to take home, which will of course be enjoyed by Bob.

Bob has been away for a few days and I look forward to seeing him when I get home tonight.

I'm a little emotionally exhausted when I finally leave the office for my drive to Langley. Langley, I think, that's a long way to go for a healing session. I wonder what it will be like. I love horses so I am excited. I hope I won't be disappointed. Sitting in traffic on Hwy 1 listening to Goyte "Somebody that I used to know" brings back memories of sitting by the pool on The Pacific Jewel on our way to the South Pacific this past February. I was well then. I was happy then. Oh what an amazing holiday we had. Come on Michelle, back to the present. Everything is going to be okay.

It is a long drive to the barn but eventually I pull up to the gates thirty minutes early. I enter the code and drive through to the barn itself. Hmmm no one here, oh well I'll sit and relax for a few minutes. It is peaceful here; the horses are watching me, vaguely interested. Up ahead I see a door for what looks like a little office, perhaps I'll go and wait in there. Upon entering I see a registration/waiver form waiting on a chair so I sit down to fill it out. The room is small and inviting, there are couches and chairs, and an easel with a large notepad on it filled with notes from a past session. I know they hold group meetings here and I'm glad it's only me. I don't know what exactly I am in for, however I do know I would not wish to do this in a group setting.

Eventually Linda arrives. Linda-Ann is a Master Coach and Intuitive Healer. Her company Unbridling

Your Brilliance does sessions involving the use of horses in healing, I wonder if this will actually help me? Am I going to get anything out of this? Linda looks normal, thank goodness. I'm glad she's not all dressed in hippie gowns redolent of patchouli. We begin talking, she is concise, calm and intelligent, I like her but how am I going to tell her what is going on with me.

"Tell me a little bit about why you are here?" she asks.

I fidget in my chair, "Um, because well, I recently got diagnosed with cancer and I'm not sure how to accept it," I say, tears streaming down my face. "I mean, I know I have it, but it's just not quite settled in me yet. I feel blocked, there is something I need to release and I don't know what it is". Damn it Michelle, you're sounding like a weirdo now.

"Okay" Linda says, "How do you feel?"

Breathing in deeply I give this some thought, "I feel sad, angry, you know, I have young children and a husband I promised I would grow old with and well, I feel like I'm not going to be able to do all this. I just feel like there is something stuck inside me. Sorry, sorry for crying like this, I just want to get it all out and heal".

"How is your family handling your illness?" Linda asks.

"My husband is amazing, he takes care of me and he's gentle and loving and so supportive and my daughter is great. She is kind and spends time with me, she doesn't like my bald head, but she's getting used to it. It's my son.

You see he doesn't want to be with me, he is embarrassed by me. I ask him to spend the night at my house and he won't. It makes me sad, sorry," sob, "I know he loves me, he just can't handle it."

"Tell me about you being Type A" Linda says, "You mentioned in the beginning that you were very Type A".

"Oh," I say, "well there was the time in 2007 that we went to Disney World as a family and I scheduled all the rides etc. in my blackberry so we could maximize our time and my husband was concerned that if something went wrong I'd be upset, and something did go wrong, both the kids got very ill, but I didn't get upset, I adapted and we made other plans".

"You're not Type A" she said, "You have good fire energy, but not too much fire energy because you were okay when things didn't work out. Too much fire energy is not healthy, yours seems well balanced". Linda takes a moment and breathes. "I am getting a message that you need to forgive".

Oh right I remember, Linda is a channeller, she gets messages and passes them on, but forgive? "Forgive whom I say?"

"I don't know" she says, "maybe someone you know, maybe forgive yourself, it's not clear I'm just getting a very strong message that you need to forgive someone."

"Okay," I say.

"Are you ready to meet the horses?" Linda asks.

"Yes, yes I'm ready, but please stay close to me as I

may be a little nervous."

We walk out to the coral, "I'm a little scared Linda, but I'll try to hide it."

"No" she says, "don't hide your feelings from the horses, come as you are, and let them know you as you are."

Walking into the coral I feel the energy of the strong beasts. They look at me, a stranger in their midst. "Please be nice," I'm thinking, "No kicking or biting please."

"We will meet each horse individually," Linda says.

The first of six horses approaches me and I take some time to get to know her. She is big, dark and has hairy feet. I feel nervous but eventually touch her and spend a few minutes getting to know her. Then she slowly walks off and we approach the next horse. This continues until I've met all but the "dominant horse", who stays in a different section of the coral. Suddenly I notice all the horses but the dominant one are around me, not too close for me to be scared, but they are standing around me watching me.

"I'd like you to breathe deeply a few times" Linda says, "one of the horses will choose to be your healer."
"Alright," I say without a clue as to what that means. I breathe deeply a few times and relax and then sure as God made little apples, a horse starts walking towards me.

"Oh my, what am I supposed to do?" I think. I stand still and this horse walks right up to me and with his nose starts rubbing my right breast all over. What the heck, how does he know? He's rubbing and rubbing, ever so gently for a horse, but firmly to me. All over my right breast and nuzzling under my right armpit where there is cancer in my lymph nodes and along my right ribcage where the cancer has spread. I can't believe this. Tears are streaming down my face, I am sobbing and sobbing and he keeps doing this, healing me. I can feel it, and he (Rio is his name) isn't stopping. Maybe Rio knows when it's done? I don't know but this feels unbelievable. Now he lifts his head and looks at me but does not move.

"Would you like to do some mutual healing," Linda asks. "Yes" I say, so she shows me how to put one hand on his heart and one hand up on his spine. I lean into Rio and we hug together, our energies passing through each other. I can feel his heart beat, I am breathing his breath, and we are one. My body is strengthening as his energy passes through me, I feel calm, my breast has softened and I feel it's part of us both, not an alien enemy on my body.

Rio and I stand together like this for what feels like an eternity, then just a quickly as it began, I feel the flow stop, we are finished, I step back and look at him, in awe. What just happened is one of the most powerful things I have every experienced.

My tears have stopped and I feel as light as air. Something has changed, something has lifted from me.

"How do you feel?" asks Linda.

"Amazing, I can't believe that just happened. How did he know?" As we walk back into the little office Linda says she has something to tell me about Rio.

"He has cancer," she says.

"Oh, is that why he was the one who chose me?" I ask.

"Maybe." Linda has me pull a card from a deck of cards; I pull a card that has an owl and a horse on it. It says I need to slow down and be more vulnerable. Interesting.

We finish up the session and I ask if I can come again. This is mind blowing and I will never forget it. I begin the long drive home a different person than the one who arrived there two hours earlier. I am physically and emotionally drained but it feels good. By the time I get home I can barely keep my eyes open and it's only five-thirty. I know this experience has changed something for me and drawn something out of me; I cannot quite put my finger on it, however I am grateful. I am grateful for Rio, grateful for finding this retreat and for allowing myself to drive out there and do it.

I lie down in bed feeling oddly at peace, a little smile plays across my face as I drift off to sleep thinking, "Two more healthy, happy days until my next chemo session so I'm going to make sure I enjoy them."

As is the case with good times, they fly a lot faster than bad times and now here I am again. It is chemo time this morning. Bob and I have to get up very early because they booked me an eight-thirty session. I am scared on the drive in, very scared to have this chemo session. It is the last one before they install the Port-a-Cath and I am wondering if my veins will fail. I arrive and reluctantly lie down on the bed for treatment, Bob as always by my side holding my hand.

As usual, the first dose of choice was my Tiger's Blood. It's rushing into my body and hunting out the cancer. It's going to eat it all away for me and then it's going to excrete it in the form of red pee...lovely. I don't like watching the Tiger's Blood go in because I know it's so scary and anything can happen. It is a long process. I am also hopped up on twelve milligrams of Decadron, a massive steroid - even two milligrams is high for me, so needless to say, the next few days shall be interesting. The unfortunate thing about today's chemo session is that I am not early enough to get a bed, and with my short body, the big chairs are quite uncomfortable. I do manage though and the nurse was lovely.

After the Tiger's Blood I have an IV drip of healing potion that I imagine going throughout the body to check to make sure Tiger didn't miss anything. The process itself is not very painful; however now, three hours later, my legs ache and feel like they each weigh two hundred pounds, so walking to the washroom is a true test of determination. The same goes for my hands - they are dead weights and typing is taking forever.

I get some good news at the clinic, my lymph nodes (from touch) appear a lot better, if not one hundred percent clear, at least ninety-five percent clear. Also the large tissue mass that was the cancer has reduced to about the size of grapefruit (maybe a little bigger) and it is softening, so good changes are being seen. I believe the combination of chemo, my attitude, my support, my alternative supplements and my alternative treatments along with my daily meditations are helping me fight this fight. My goal is to be cancer free. So when they go to operate or radiate there will be very little to be found. Now that is a great goal.

Five hours later and I am home and a walking zombie. I feel like I am in "The Hunger Games", I've been poked and prodded and my personal groomers have pumped me full of new fangled stuff to make me a better fighter.

Now, I have been thrown into the Arena, with nothing but an iPhone, nausea meds and a loving husband for armour. Five days of fighting, but I'll be the victor wearing the crown at the end, I promise. Just don't throw too many weird storms, fires, Flacker Jackets or Ghouls at me and I'll be fine.


Apparently I was mistaken about being fine. Today is day six after my third round of chemotherapy. This has been a tough round again. I have heard that it gets worse as you go along because the drugs build up in your system and the side affects accumulate. I guess I just didn't want to believe it. I've been keeping a very low profile this time around and haven't been entertaining any visitors. The Oasis, my backyard paradise has been closed while I skulk around the house from room to room trying to keep from vomiting and making sure a toilet is always nearby. I'm not in a "feeling sorry for myself" mode. I'm in a "I feel really shitty and this sucks" kind of mode. Once again the questions of how can I continue with this and how the hell will I handle it when cancer raises its ugly head again - assuming I can become symptom free this time around, are going through my head.

When one first faces cancer it's all new, so you have no idea of what you are in for, but once you get through a few chemo sessions and you're looking down the long road to recovery, then it becomes a living hell. A few days ago I started watching (and then stopped after three episodes) a program called The Walking Dead. I didn't enjoy the show very much but there was a line said by the main character Rick in the first episode that really hit home. He said he felt like he was living a nightmare and was sure he would wake up, until he realized it wasn't a nightmare. It was real, this was life now. That is how I feel having a serious life threatening cancer. Sometimes I wake up in the middle of the night and still think it must not be true, surely it is all just a bad dream. I feel like I am one of the Walking Dead.

Many people have had cancer and travelled this road before me and I had no idea how hard it was for them. When you get cancer you do become one of the Walking Dead and no matter what you do, or how much money you have, it isn't easy. I mean look at Steve Jobs, he had all the money in the world and I bet his treatments were just as horrible and he suffered just as much as anyone else. There is no getting off this track once you are on it. You have to just continue walking, plodding and sometimes crawling through each treatment, each session, each day with the hopes that you will at the end leave the 'Walking Dead' and become one of the 'Living in Limbo's.' Yes, not living, but 'Living in Limbo' because this nasty disease looms over you for the rest of your life, so you are never normal again. You can never just do anything you want and not worry that it will bring back the cancer. Those days of drinking a bottle of bubbly without a care in the world are long gone. I will forever be worrying if I'm triggering the cancer or if the sugar in the alcohol is feeding a tiny little cancer devil in some other part of my body that will eventually raise its ugly head with a resounding "Gotcha Sucka!" Perhaps this is punishment for not eating my greens. I've never liked greens and now I have to eat so many of them I feel like a rabbit gorging on a garden and it makes me ill. YUK! Life was not meant for greens, it was meant for champagne and oysters followed by a damn good steak with a damn good Cabernet and topped off with Crème Brulée and Cognac. Oh and did I mention all of this being served to you on some tropical island by some snooty waiter while you sit in your ten thousand dollar Versace dress. Now that's the life. I guess if I had a defined amount of time to live and a massive amount of money I would do just that until I wasn't well enough to cut and eat my own steak. Then I'd get the French waiter to serve me champagne and happy pills until I saw the other side. Oh it's so nice to sit here at the Oasis and fantasize about all this. I haven't felt like hurling in at least ten minutes. As a matter of fact the only irritating thing is my left arm from the Vitamin C IV I had yesterday.

I had received the okay from Sasha to proceed with Vitamin C IV therapy and yesterday was the first day. It was a disaster. Dr. Ash, a local naturopath, was lovely, no concerns there, and did her best to make me feel at ease. I sat in a little room watching her fill an IV bag of Vitamin C with about six or seven other medications including B12 complex, magnesium, trace minerals...and on and on. I don't remember most of them, just that it was freaking me out. While she was doing this my left arm was heating up, getting ready to be assaulted. The first needle to go in was a charm, not much pain and in a good vein, so Dr. A injected the yellow medicine, then attached the IV line. It was, as I was getting comfortable, that the trouble began. The needle, which was in the crook of my arm, slipped out of the vein, so, the IV infusion was now going into my body not my vein. "Damn!" That hurt like you wouldn't believe. Finally we stopped the IV and tried to jiggle the needle back into the vein, with no luck, the more we jiggled the worse it got, so out came the needle and on went the heating pad to prep me for another one. This one wasn't so good, the vein was smaller and it hurt a lot going in, then it hurt the entire hour that I sat there with the fluid dripping into me. It also creates the most disgusting metallic taste in your mouth and there is a horrendous smell, similar to the smell you get if you open a tightly sealed vitamin bottle and stick your nose in it. Try it, you won't be impressed. I left there wondering if I really can go through with this twice a week. I was nauseous and had a massive headache going in and left feeling even worse. This stuff is supposed to boost my immune system and help keep the cancer at bay, so taking it is the right thing to do. I'm just going to have to figure out how the hell I can manage it. With chemo, I don't have a choice, I have to go, but with this I do have a choice so I'll have to muster all my strength every couple of days and just suck it up. I am getting my Port-a-Cath installed on August 7th, and will ask if we can use that to administer the Vitamin C IV. Wouldn't that be great? See lots of silver linings here. Speaking of silver linings I had a little laugh with my girlfriend Lisa, when she stopped by with banana bread yesterday, about how this was the craziest weight loss program ever. I can think of many easier ways to lose those last five pounds, however this one worked like a charm.

Today I am really struggling with nausea and as I get up from the couch in the Oasis I can feel a wave of it hit me. I took a heavy anti nausea drug this morning, which seemed to keep things steady; mind you I haven't done much yet. Funnily enough, one of my nausea drugs is the same drug they give to Schizophrenics, so I decided to avoid that one for now.

My sister Marie called this afternoon. Apparently mum said she has brain cancer. I was completely shocked to hear this. The last time I had spoken to mum she said she wasn't feeling very well and was suffering from what she called "sudden deaf syndrome". Mum said she would be sitting in her chair and suddenly she would lose her hearing in her left ear. I thought this to be very odd. However I did not pay too much attention to it because my entire life mum has been complaining about some or other ailment. We three children are quite used to this and simply nod and express our concern when mum discusses any of her many health issues.

Marie said that mum was going to go to the doctor tomorrow to review the results of her CT Scan and to discuss her brain cancer. This certainly sounded a little more serious, so Marie decided she was going to take the ferry over to the coast and join mum at her doctor's appointment. I asked her to call me when it was done, although to be honest I was quite sure it was probably not brain cancer, just some lesions they had found that were nothing to worry about.



I didn't let it dwell too heavily on my mind last night, and this morning I am busy getting things organized for our little holiday. We have decided to take the kids to Las Vegas for five days next week. Bob's daughter Anna is coming with us and has even offered to spend an evening with Kory and Rose so that Bob and I can have a night out.  We have not told Kory and Rose about the holiday and plan on surprising them next week.  I have my Port-a-Cath surgery on Tuesday and am spending the rest of the week at my dad's place.  Kory has a baseball camp so will be staying with my sister and her husband, and then on Friday Bob will drive in with Rose.

I spend the rest of the day organizing a house sitter and researching teenage friendly activities in Las Vegas.  At around four o'clock the phone rings, it is Marie.

"Hello", I say.

"Hi, it's me.  I'm at mum's.  We just got back from the doctors office." Marie says.

"How is she," I ask.

"Mum has brain cancer," Marie says, her voice hitching slightly

"What? How do they know? What do you mean?" I ask, confused.

"She has lots of lesions on her brain," Marie says. "It is advanced, some of the tumours are quite large."

I am silent.

"The doctor says they are going to order a full body CT Scan, he doesn't believe the cancer started in the brain, he thinks it has metastasized there" Marie says.

I am so shocked.  I don't really know what to say. "When are they doing the next scan?" I ask.

"He has ordered it but it may take a few weeks to get in," Marie says.

"Did he give any treatment plan or prognosis?" I ask.

"Mum doesn't want to do chemo," Marie says "and the doctor said it looks pretty advanced. She has maybe four months, maybe six."

"I can understand mum not wanting to do chemo. She had to look after me during one of my treatment weeks and has seen how it ravages the body" I said. "I can't imagine going through chemotherapy at her age."

"I am going to stay here with mum for a few days. Do you want to talk to her?" Marie asks.

"Yes please." She puts mum on the phone. I don't really know what to say.

"Mum," I say, "I'm so sorry, are you okay?"

"Yes," she says, as calm as can be. "This is why I was going deaf, the tumours were pressing on the hearing area in my brain."

"Does it hurt?" I ask.

"No, I just go deaf, and also lately I've been falling a bit and the doctor thinks the tumours could be doing that too." She says.

This didn't make sense to me, but then I don't know anything about brain tumours. We speak a little longer, and then she puts Marie back on the line. Marie and the doctor suspect mum's falling is because she is having seizures from the pressure on her brain. That is why she is staying for a while, to keep an eye on mum.

"Have you told Sean yet?" I ask.

"No," Marie says.

"I'll call him," I say. Sean will be devastated. He and mum have become very close in the last five years. I know at first he won't believe it, he will need the proof, but the proof is there. Marie has copies of the CT scan of mum's brain and it speaks specifically to the number and size of all the tumours. This is for real. I wonder what kind of universe this is that would give both mum and I cancer at the same time. I do understand her not wanting treatment however I don't quite believe or understand the short time frame she has been given.

I am too shocked to cry. I just sit there after we hang up the phone, staring blankly at the wall across the room. It does not compute, does not resonate. How can mum have advanced brain cancer? She was here not so long ago looking after me. She was fit as a fiddle and looked great. Surely there is a mistake, after all they didn't do any biopsies, and maybe these tumours are benign.

The call to Sean goes poorly, as was expected. He is shocked and upset. I wanted to tell him not to worry too much, but how can I say that when I've just told him that mum has cancer. He said he would call her later this evening and go over in a few days to visit her. Sean has asked if Kory and Rose can come and spend the weekend with him near the end of August so that he can take them out on his boat. I agreed to play this by ear, depending on how mum was doing. As I am only a week post chemo, I am not well enough to make the trip over to see her yet, and next week I will be away. I have to try and figure out a time to go over because as soon as I get back I go in for chemo once again. Cancer certainly keeps me busy.

## THE HIGHS AND THE LOWS

Today is Port-a-Cath day.  I wake up at five-thirty to get ready.  Wendy will be here shortly and although I am nervous I am looking forward to having the port and giving my poor veins a break.

Wendy knocks as I'm brushing my teeth.

"Ready?" she asks

"Give me a minute," I say, my mouth full of toothpaste.  I rush back upstairs, finish brushing my teeth, put a nice hat on my baldhead and in minutes we are off out the door.

Wendy always goes in to work early and was kind enough to offer to drop me off at the hospital for the surgery.  I am not used to being up this early anymore, so am not much of a conversationalist on the drive in.  Besides, I am too nervous to focus much anyway.

We arrive at Lions Gate at seven-fifteen.  Wendy wishes me luck and I head on down to the basement of the hospital where all the big machines are.  I check in at the reception desk and a lovely nurse brings me to a hospital bed located in a large room with four beds and a nursing station.

"I am really scared," I say.

"You don't need to be," she says.  We do these all week long and the radiologist is very good."

"Radiologist?" I ask.  "You mean it's not an actual surgeon?"

"No, and you aren't going under a general anesthetic. We will provide you with a sedative, however it is only local anesthetic" she says.

Now I am really scared. "I'm going to be awake for this?" I ask.

"Yes, but you will be fine, really" she says reassuringly.

"Can I have an Ativan please?" I ask.

She brings me an Ativan and a few minutes later comes around to hook me up to an IV. I beg my veins to co-operate as I watch her slide the needle into my arm. She is very good at it, gets the vein her first try and I hardly feel a thing.

After a few minutes she comes back and rolls my bed into the operating room. There are three nurses, an anesthetist and a technician in the room already. They transfer me to the surgical bed and then begin setting things up.

First they position me properly on the bed, then they begin to position all this massive machinery around me and then they hook things up to both my fingers. I know one is for Oxygen SAT levels, but I'm not sure what the other one is for. It is quite intimidating. I am lying there watching this huge seventy-inch TV screen, which is what the radiologist will use to see inside my body to make sure he is inserting the little rubber tube into my jugular vein and not accidentally somewhere else. This screen also shows my heart rate, blood pressure, Oxygen SAT levels, and some other measurements that I cannot recognize.

It is bloody intimidating lying here with all this stuff going on around me. I thought this was supposed to be pretty simple surgery. At least I can see the TV and watch my heart rate, so I start playing this little game where I try to slow my heart rate down - it isn't working. Then things get ugly. One of the nurses comes and cleans my chest and my neck all over with a sterile solution, and then she puts this huge drape sheet over my head. It has a hole in it with sticky sides that stick to my chest and neck, leaving an opening for the doc to get at, and the rest of it lies across my head. It is making me feel very claustrophobic. I just about have a fit until they get a little gadget and place it just above my head and put the sheet across it so it is not covering my face.

Finally the Doctor arrives. He walks around to where I can see a tiny area of the room and introduces himself. Although I can only see a fraction of his face, he looks old enough and competent enough to do this. Here we go...he starts poking and prodding my chest, I guess checking for muscle mass and to find the correct spot.

"We're going to start," he says.

"Excuse me. Start? I'm still awake. Where are the sedatives?" I ask. "Hello," I am thinking, "Remember me, the person you are about to cut into. I'm not some super human pain-loving freak. I need meds."

"Okay" he says, "We have given you some already, but we will give you some more."

"Thank You" I say, relieved.

So they comply and give me something via the IV that makes me feel all soft and nice all over, so he starts injecting my chest with the needles.

"No wait! Stop, I can still feel you.  More meds please," I say.  This isn't what I expected, I don't want to feel the needles and I certainly don't want to feel the scalpel as it cuts into my skin.

He must have requested more medication because all I feel is the prick, prick of more needles in the neck and chest and then suddenly I'm gone.  La La Land.

I wake up to the lovely nurse smiling at me and I'm in the recovery area and it's done.  Phew, all done, and really not so bad, just tender, but then I guess I'm still numb.

"How did it go", I ask.

"Just great, no problems at all," she says.  Oh lucky me, it's done, over with and it wasn't nearly as scary as I thought.  I take a little peek down to my chest but I can't see anything other than two big bandages.  One just on my lower neck and one in the middle of my chest to the left hand side with a bump under it about the size of half a Ping-Pong ball.  It is like having a little alien being inside you.  I'm going to call him Mork.  He's going to save my veins from collapse and make chemo and blood drawing so much easier.

A short while later my father picks me up.  I am still a bit drowsy and when we get back to his house I go to sleep for a few hours.  When I awaken before dinner Mork, my little alien, and the other incision site in my neck are throbbing. I am glad I am not going anywhere for a few days. I can just relax here and be looked after until we go to Las Vegas.

I am attending a cancer educational session for three days, tomorrow being the first day. It is only a two-block walk from dad and Tina's house so no long drives needed. Although sleep is very uncomfortable, I manage with the help of a little sleep aid and some Advil to finally get there.

It is Friday, the week is over and Mork feels a little better. I take a quick peek in the mirror, the wound still has a long way to go to heal, but looks a lot nicer than it did a few days ago. I am waiting for Bob and the children to come and pick me up. We have told them we will be spending the weekend in a hotel in the city, something we used to do for fun quite a bit a few years ago.

I learned a lot this week, but most of it frustrated me. I already knew that some cancers such as Ovarian Cancer and (Regular) Breast Cancer could be hereditary. Things in your environment like asbestos can cause some cancers and then there are those cancers caused by abusing your body through smoking or alcohol. It's not as if these cancers are any better or worse than what I have, it's just that if I got a cancer due to genetic history or abuse, well then perhaps I could understand it a little more.

What challenges me is that I've always taken pretty good care of myself - yes I like my wine but otherwise I have lived a healthy life. I've never smoked, I don't do recreational drugs, I don't eat junk food (okay once in a blue moon), and I have always exercised - yet I got cancer. I think this is totally insane, and to make matters worse, I didn't get a slow growing Breast Cancer or an easily curable cancer, no, I got a virulent, hard to treat cancer.

I also learned ways to help fight cancer and how to prevent it from recurring. What did all these wonderfully wise people say? Eat well, exercise, drink lots of water and you'll heal and you will keep cancer from recurring. Does anyone else see the irony here? That is what I have always done. I've been shown all these stats about how if you exercise three to five hours per week you can prevent breast cancer recurrence by as much as forty-five percent, and if you eat cruciferous vegetables then you can reduce mortality by sixty-two percent and recurrence by thirty-five percent. I understand that if I've been a couch potato, junk food junky, but for me, that isn't much of a change, so what does that mean?

What can I change that will help me? I think the only thing would be for me to slow down and not live such a high energy, stressful life. The problem with that is that I love my work and the stress I put myself under to achieve. I'm not sure what I would do with my time if I weren't so driven. Is there another way to live? I am going to have to try and find out. For now, I'm just going to relax and try to enjoy a few days away with my family.

We arrive at the Delta Airport Hotel in time to enjoy a nice dinner outside on the patio. It is just the four of us tonight; Anna is meeting us at the airport tomorrow. Kory and Rose still don't have a clue, which is exciting for me. By ten I am exhausted, my port Mork is aching and I need some sleep. So I go to bed early while the rest of the family stay up to enjoy the hotel.

I awaken to the light of the sun streaming into the room. Bob is already awake, sitting quietly in the bed beside me. I tell Bob I'm going to tell the kids that we are going to go to a shopping mall today, but since we are going to check out of this particular room, we need to take our bags with us. Odd, I know, but I cannot think of another way to get them on a bus to the airport. The idea of going shopping would definitely work.

We wake them up and an hour later we are in the lobby waiting for the bus to the mall. As the bus pulls up, Kory, ever the observant teenager asks me why the bus says Airport on it.

"I'm not sure." I say, "maybe it stops at the airport first."

He looks at me queerly. I'm not sure he believes me.

A few minutes later it arrives at the airport. We get off, walk into the main concourse and I pull out the tickets.

"Guess what guys? We are going to Las Vegas," I say.

They look at me in shock, and then squeal in joy. Oh how I love this feeling, I love the happy looks on their faces. They have both wanted to go to Las Vegas for so long. I am so glad we are able to do this for them.

"Anna is also coming," I say.

"Yippee!" Rose says. "Can I share the room with her?"

We have two rooms, because we have three adults, so it is decided that Rose and Anna will share and Kory will be with us.

The flight is uneventful. Bob and I sit together and Anna sits with Kory and Rose. When we arrive the kids are literally bouncing off the walls with excitement. The first signs we are in Vegas are the banks of slot machines running down the center of the airport causeway. Rose wants to try one out so I have to explain to her that you have to be an adult to gamble and so therefore she cannot play the slots, thank goodness. Retrieving our baggage is quick and easy and soon we are walking towards the exit to find a taxi to take us to our hotel.

The hot Vegas air hits us like a wave as we slide out through the exit doors. It is stifling. Vegas in August is not for the faint of heart. My cellphone weather app tells me it is forty-two degrees Celsius and I can feel the heat like an overly warm blanket tucked too tightly around me. Thankfully it is only a few minutes wait for a taxi. We pile in and head off ready for our first view of Sin City.

It does not disappoint. On our way to our hotel we pass by The Excalibur, Mandalay Bay, the Luxor and we can see New York New York in the distance. Further down the road stand the gleaming tower from the Paris hotel.  This is exactly what the kids were expecting and the cameras are going off like crazy.    We arrive at the doors to The Tropicana bubbling over with excitement.  A brief moment of overwhelming heat hits us as we unload the taxi and walk inside to check in.

We were unable to get adjoining rooms, but are just down the hall from each other and each has a lovely view of the pool.  That is the first place I want to go.  I love to swim, but due to the Port-a-Cath I am not allowed to swim at all, just a little lower body wading.  I cannot resist enjoying it a little, so we get on our swimsuits and head down to the pool deck.  It is five-thirty Las Vegas time and still sweltering.  Anna and I share a Pina Colada, a fourteen-dollar Pina Colada, and sit in a shady spot near the edge of the pool.  I feel this tremendous urge to throw caution to the wind and jump right into the water with the kids, but the thought of having complications with Mork while I am in the United States and having to spend any time in a hospital down here is enough to dampen that desire.

After dinner that night we take a walk down the strip.  It is wild and crazy and Rose won't let go of my hand for the first little while.  Then she sees Kory sauntering along enjoying it all so runs up to join him.  For me the walk down the strip proves to be too much.  It's not just my exhaustion from chemo and the port just recently installed.  It's also the heat.  I find it unbearable in my current state.  Somehow the chemo drugs make me more sensitive to temperature extremes and this is too much for me.  We decide to rent a car the next day so that we can at least drive up and down the strip as well as go to The Hoover Dam and Freemont Street.

The following day is spent enjoying the strip again, this time doing some shopping.  Then we head back to the hotel for some pool time, well, all of us except Kory enjoy some pool time.  Rose and Anna swim for quite a while and Bob and I sit in deck chairs enjoying a couple of cold drinks.  Bob likes Pina Coladas so he has no problem keeping cool.  I prefer a cold beer.  The trouble is that in this heat the beer is warm within five minutes.  Soon it is time to head up to the room to get ready for the Tournament of Kings show at the Excalibur.

When I was in London in 1985 I had been to a Shakespearean dinner theater that I found fantastic.  It was in the basement of an ancient building, all stone walls and an ancient well-worn brick floor.  There was a center area surrounded by alcoves, which were entered via archways.  Candles lighted the space and the alcoves were mostly pitch black, off in the distance.  It made you feel as if you were really in the Middle Ages.  The furniture was sparse and old.  There were two long tables with benches.  The guests sat at these tables and were served by the performers.  There were no utensils so all eating was by hand.  The grog was poured from ancient looking tankards and the meal was served on metal plates.  All the while an exciting theatre production was going on around you, the actors involving members of the audience in their manipulative schemes to achieve domination over their rivals.  It was one of my most memorable experiences from my trip to London, and although I certainly wasn't expecting Vegas to match up, I was hoping for something similar.

Right from the start I knew it would be different. We were all seated in a large oval area with what looked like a dressage arena in the middle.    We had a long bench in front of the seats where the food and drink were delivered.  The servers in our section were very prompt, but the wine left a lot to be desired.  Although the atmosphere was not even close, the entertainers put on a great show, involved the audience throughout and by the end even I was impressed. We all felt it had been a fun evening and I for one was ready to pass out with exhaustion.  The kids and I went to bed and Bob and Anna went out to check out some nightlife.

The next day we go to The Hoover Dam, which is a long trip.  The air-conditioning in the car cannot keep up with the burning Nevadan heat so the car is lukewarm inside.  We have to park one or two kilometers from the entrance to the dam.  Normally this would not be an issue, but today is not a normal day.  It is close to fifty degrees Celsius and we have to walk this long way along a concrete walkway.  Thank goodness there is a washroom halfway there.  I go inside, whip off my shirt and hat and soak them in the sink.  This helps tremendously, I encourage the kids to do the same because I can see they too are fading, but they think it is a stupid idea.  By the time we get to the entrance, my shirt has already dried. Now that is heat.

We enjoy the tour very much.  The air-conditioning throughout is a big plus, and two hours later were on our way back to Las Vegas.  Over the next few days we see the Mob Museum, Freemont Street, Circus Circus and of course the famous Pawn Stars pawn shop that Kory had been asking to go to.  By the time Wednesday rolls around and it is time to go home I am broke and exhausted.  Las Vegas may be inexpensive to fly to from Vancouver, and the hotels are reasonable but the food and drink are not.  I am sure we spent more than our entire flight and hotel bill on food, if not more.  I am not very impressed and cannot say I am in a rush to go back soon.  As a matter of fact, I am so exhausted I am actually looking forward to my chemo session tomorrow morning.  It is to be my last of the A/C protocol, which has been so brutal for me.  I cannot wait for it to be over.

## A DEATH IN THE FAMILY

It is Saturday morning and I'm sitting in bed with my Waldo trying to get the energy up to go to the local farmers market and see what fresh organic food might await me. I am so happy to be past my last Adriamycin/Cyclophosphamide chemo cocktail. This time it was so much easier because I had made the decision to have Mork (the Port-a-Cath) installed last week. For anyone facing long chemotherapy treatment times like I am, I highly recommend getting it installed. I was terrified to get one done. I mean, who really wants to have a foreign object installed right on your chest and then fed directly into your jugular vein? That being said, Mork has proven to be amazing. I hardly felt the needle going in, wasn't worried about a vein failing and certainly wasn't worried about the IV missing my vein and pouring Tiger's Blood (Adriamycin) directly under my skin.

One unfortunate side effect (at least I'm calling it a side-effect) from this chemo session is a morbid sense of sadness. I have been trying to avoid support groups and reading any statistics about Inflammatory Breast Cancer because they are just too unacceptable for me but yesterday an invitation came across my Facebook to attend 'An afternoon discussion on Inflammatory Breast Cancer: An update for patients and the community and a look towards the future.' So I went online to read a little more about it, as their clinic is part of MD Anderson

Medical Centre and they specialize in IBC, so therefore they are the experts on IBC. What was the first thing that stood out for me?

### INFLAMMATORY BREAST CANCER FACTS

*Inflammatory breast cancer is rare, and it is the most aggressive form of breast cancer. According to the American Cancer Society, it accounts for only 1% to 5% of all invasive breast cancers. However, the five-year overall survival rate is 40%, compared to nearly 90% for all other types of breast cancer combined.*

This threw me over the edge. I mean I'm already feeling so down from all the treatments and having so many more months of treatments to face, that to hear again, and this time from the foremost clinic for treating this cancer, that they still cannot achieve better than a forty percent survival rate over five years, well that was just a kick in the pants. Once I am done all my treatments and back to what they call 'Normal' (the next new normal), I will probably be forty-nine, so this will have already taken two years out of my life. If I were to get IBC again within three years, I'm not too sure I'd have the desire or energy to go through this all over again. What a way to live, and if it does come back, I will have no breasts for it to come back to, so where will it come back? Lymph nodes? Bones? My brain? I have heard that HER2+ IBC, the kind that I have metastasizes to the brain. How will that be?

NO NO NO! This cannot happen. I need my strength and my belief back, my belief that I can and will fight this and it will never happen to me again. I need to work on the inner being, more to build up faith and a strong resilience. If the medicine cannot heal me, then my mind will just have to do the job. I have so much more life to live and two lovely children to raise (I want to be able to see the day they stop fighting with each other), and I also want to educate people about IBC so that they can catch it early, be their own advocates and not listen to their doctors when they tell them it's nothing, just a spider bite, or mastitis. By catching it early and avoiding the six or more weeks of back and forth with doctors, you can save your life.

I don't want this to happen to anyone else. It's not a fun ride to be on. Speaking of rides, I think I'll try a little ride around the block on my cruiser bike - it's about the only thing that's managing to keep my spirits up these days. I give Waldo a little shove off the bed.

"Up we get lazy bones," I say. "Time for us to get some exercise."

Unfortunately my little excursion yesterday didn't do much to boost my spirits. Today I'm like a zombie, just part of the walking dead, tears streaming down my face walking from room to room just hoping that by putting one step in front of the other I can get through this. Walk down to the laundry with dirty shirts, pick up some clean clothes, bring them up to Kory's room. Have a breakdown and cry on his bed, get back up I see some clothes left in the suitcase from Vegas. I should walk those down to the laundry. I can barely see through the tears. Put them in the tub, turn it on. Stop, breathe, pick up some clean towels and bring them back upstairs. I can do this. I can do this, one step at a time.

I had no idea this would be so hard. I have lost my way, lost my purpose in all this. I used to have some value. I got up every day for a reason. I had a job I loved. I was independent and happy. Now the days drag by like a living hell. I have no reason anymore; I am just a burden, just doing what I am supposed to do with nothing there for me except worry. I don't even know if I will make it to the other side and when I do, what is there? Who am I? How will I get back on my feet again? I am so torn apart by all this. As I sit here on my bedroom floor I can see photographs of my little ones when they were very little. I have failed them. I am sorry. I was not supposed to get sick. I am the strong one. My babies... I love them so much. Then there is the wedding photo of my husband and me with the horses. He is my rock - I recall our wedding song, "Hero" by Enrique Iglesias.

I had no idea that Bob would have to be my hero. That I would put him through so much, it's just not fair, not right. I need to stand on my own two feet but I don't know how. If I can just cry all the tears out, then there will be nothing left to cry and I'll be better, cleansed maybe. It's early though, around five in the evening and the dog has to be fed, and I have to be fed and I'm so bad at doing that, and then there is the long night ahead of me.

However, it's not just one long night, it is many many more long nights as I fight through this. It will be months and months of ups and downs. Do I have the resilience to get me through? I know I have to because I have people counting on me, but sometimes...well sometimes it's just so bloody hard.

Up I get, eyes swollen and the dog has come upstairs looking to be fed - at least that is a purpose. So I'll make another trip back down the stairs, feed the dog, open the fridge door, look inside, see nothing I like, close the fridge door and go and sit on the couch until something else motivates me to move. Never fear, I'm okay - it's just one step at a time.

On and on the days drag, and all of them much the same. Today is day six past my chemo session and the side effects this time are by far worse than before. I had been told that the affects are cumulative and that each time you will feel worse, for longer, but well, quite frankly I guess I didn't want to believe it. As I sit here with the most disgusting tasting metal mouth, sores all over my mouth and throat, nausea, depression and an inability to taste anything, I wonder can it get any worse. I also wonder, does it ever get any better? Is there light at the end of this long, dark tunnel? Since I don't have any answers I reach out to a few people who would.

I speak to Terry; probably one of the biggest IBC Education advocates in the United States, as well as to Suzanne, a Canadian woman who was first diagnosed in 2009. I learn a few things I didn't know and also learn a few things I do not want to know. For example, IBC has been around for about 100 years? Certain cancer agencies refuse to put warnings up about it because by the time women find out it is too late and there is no cure. Imagine that. Not letting people know that something so deadly exists because you have no answers. I know there is no "test" yet for IBC, but there is a big difference in prognosis to find out at a stage III rather than at stage IV (IBC always presents at stage III or IV). Normal cancer cells reproduce every one hundred days or so, IBC cells reproduce almost daily so catching it as early as possible is important.

Terry is a five-year IBC survivor and has had NED (no evidence of disease) for those five years as well. She said she is part of a small group, but women are living longer with IBC and she knows some women who have been as long as nine years. It takes a while for all this to settle with me, and I can guarantee it's still not settled, but what I do know is this. I now have an expiry date. I may live to be fifty years old - I may not. It's highly likely I won't see sixty so I might as well come to grips with this and "face it like a man". Isn't that hilarious. Am I mad? Yes! I'm extremely pissed off, frustrated, sad, angry, you name it. Those who know me know that I've always lived a large life. I have fun and am crazy and do crazy things and I love living, so I'm very pissed off that cancer has chosen me. I just want to frigging annihilate it.

Unfortunately I don't have that choice, so I have to choose how to live with it and make the best of it. Right now as I sit here feeling like a nuclear waste factory has taken root in my mouth, it's hard to be positive and enjoy things - even Haagen Dazs tastes terrible - but I know things will get better with time. They will also get a little worse over the next four rounds of chemo. I may lose my ability to type, my brain will become more fuddled than it is and the heavy doses of steroids that I'll have to start taking soon may make me go postal. Still, there will be an end to the chemo one day, radiation and surgery will take place and then hopefully I will be done. I'm going to push through the shitty times and try to keep my eye on the prize. When I am feeling better then I'm going to start enjoying more family time and take some time to do the things I've always wanted to do, even if it means moving and downsizing and cutting back on certain things. I can't waste this time now, every day counts, even if it's just a day spent sleeping to give me energy for the days that follow, I need to do it.

What I'd like most of all is to go away on a Caribbean cruise with all my friends and family after all this stress and just chill. Sit on the deck drinking bubbly, watching the sunset and laughing about the Tiger's Blood or the day my hair fell out. I want to wake in the morning to breakfast on my balcony, the smell of sea air, the sounds of my children laughing in the cabin next to me and my wonderful, kind, and amazing husband by my side. I'd like my biggest decision of my day to be whether we are going to go on the Catamaran trip with the Ellis family or Scuba diving with the Black family. I'd like to spend time walking down the streets of St. Lucia, tasting the local cuisine and haggling over souvenirs with the vendors. If I had my druthers I'd become a travel writer and go to the most amazing places, have the most amazing experiences and share them with others via the written word. Now that would truly be a great life. Just don't send me to Vegas again any time soon.

It's Friday morning. I am feeling fairly human today I think as I sit up. Perhaps I'll turn on the TV for a little morning news. Bob is away working, so I don't get my usual coffee brought to me in bed. He does spoil me, I realize.

The TV is on Global, the local station. It is eight-thirty in the morning and the news is about to start. Sophie Lui's image shows on the screen with today's top story.

"….Shooting in Coquitlam…the victim Sean Campbell…home invasion…. I hear, stunned. No, I think, no it cannot be, that's a common name, but Sean Campbell, Coquitlam. Did they say the street? No. I start screaming, No. It's not possible. A huge hollow scream is starting low in my throat.

I pause the news and realize it will have been saved automatically on my PVR and I can rewind and rewatch. I quickly do so and this is what I hear.

"Your top stories this morning - a deadly shooting in Coquitlam, our reporter Lee is on the scene in Coquitlam this morning." Sophie says.

"Sophie, they're saying that the victim Sean Campbell was shot in the entranceway of his home, about four houses down behind me late last night. It appears Campbell interrupted a burglary in progress when he arrived home at around eleven o'clock." Lee says.

I can see Sean's street and know now this is him. Tears are streaming down my face as I wail in grief, I feel as if I have been punched very hard in the middle of my chest.

"The RCMP say the home invasion may not have been random and that the victim's house may have been specifically targeted." Lee continues.

I reach for the phone to call my sister Marie, she must know by now, but why hasn't she called me I wonder? If she knows, she surely would have called. I dial her number hesitantly, sobbing as I listen to the sound of it ringing.

"Hello," Marie says.

"Hi Marie, it's me," I sob. "I guess you heard about Sean."

"No," she says. "What happened?"

I can barely contain myself, "He's been killed. Someone killed him. I just saw it on the news," I say.

Marie is quiet for a moment then she asks what happened. I tell her what I saw on the news and ask her what she thinks we should do.

"Does dad know?" she asks.

"I don't know," I say.

We talk a little longer, both of us shocked and upset. We decide that I will call dad and Marie will call mum. I cannot believe that we actually have to call our parents to tell them their son has been killed.

I know it is early in the morning however I feel certain dad is up. The phone rings twice before he picks up.

"Campbell good morning," he says as he answers the phone.

"Dad," I manage to get out. "Dad, oh dad, I am so sorry, so so sorry," I sob. My voice hitching, my heart pounding, my chest aching with the worst heartache I can imagine. Then I hear my fathers voice through my tears and I am shocked.

"Calm down dear," he says gently, "calm down, I can't understand you, what is wrong?"

It dawns on me, the shock of it, that he hasn't been told. The RCMP have not notified my father. I'm confused. Why not? But I don't have time to think about this just now. I have to tell my father that he has lost his only son, and in a horribly violent manner.

"Dad, it's Sean, he's been killed," I say. "Oh dad, I just saw it on the news, didn't anyone call you?"

"Pardon me?" he says. "What did you say?" "Sean, killed, please calm down and explain, what do you mean you saw it on the news."

I am sobbing, can barely speak. "Dad it was just on Global News. My PVR recorded it. Maybe he's not dead, maybe I heard that wrong, maybe he got shot but is still alive.  Maybe I heard it wrong," I repeat.  As I say this I turn the volume down low on my TV, rewind the piece and listen from the beginning.  They had said victim, I remember, and a victim could still be alive.

The piece plays again and I hear the keywords "deadly shooting", no, not just victim, Sean is dead, gone. "Sorry dad," I say, "I just listened to it again, it is true, he has been shot, he was at home, it was last night."

I feel hollow as I picture my father on the other end of the phone.  Why was he not informed?  This is cruel.  A father does not need to find out about the death of his son this way.  Would a two in the morning knock on the door from the RCMP have been any better?  Probably not, I don't know, this is not something either of us has experience with.

"Listen love," dad says.  "Let me come up there and get you so we can be together."

"Thanks dad, but I can manage the drive," I state. "I'm just going to shower, get the dog taken care of and then I'll head over."  My brain is reeling with thoughts. "Why did I put the TV on this morning?"  I never do that; it's not like me to ever watch the morning news.  What in the world pushed me to do so today, I wonder.

Breaking the news to Marie and dad was devastating for me.  As the eldest child I have always felt responsible for the well being of the family.  I know that is rather egotistical, but I have.  I remember as a child, if my parents were fighting I couldn't stand it.  I was so concerned with keeping everyone happy and keeping the family together. At family dinners if there was tension in the air I would act the fool to break the ice and keep the focus away from whatever mum and dad may have been arguing about. I don't know if all elder children feel it is their responsibility to keep everyone together, but for a long time I certainly felt like it was mine.

Now, I've had to call my sister and my father and tell them that their brother and son is dead. Gone. No longer a part of this living family. Our goofy little boy, who grew into a big, strong, stubborn man is now gone. His life has been taken from us and shockingly so, in the blink of an eye. He was such a funny little boy. Always trying to please everyone and wanting more than anything to be loved. Suddenly a huge wave of guilt washes over me. I was such a terrible sister to him. I used to deliberately do naughty things and blame them on Sean. I always got him into trouble and he was never quick enough to get out of it. I feel sick to the stomach. What if I'd been nicer, loved him more, would this have happened? The RCMP say this was a targeted home invasion, what if it was someone from Sean's younger years when he was an angry young man, someone with a grudge who decided to resolve it once and for all?

I realize my thoughts are ridiculous and self-focused, but I cannot help it. I have never lost anyone I have loved before, so for now, this is all about me, about the pain and loss that I am feeling. I look down at the huge pile of tissues on my lap, all soaked with snot and tears. This is insane, I have to get a hold of myself, and I have to be strong for everyone. Slowly I pull myself together, pick up the phone and dial my Bob's cell number.

One hour later I am in my car on the way to my father's. It is a hot late summer morning and the world outside looks beautiful, but I could not give a damn. This is the hardest drive I have ever done down the Sea to Sky highway. My vision is completely blurred by tears and three times I have to pull over, my body wracked with sobs, to calm myself down before continuing. The pain is unbelievable. I keep thinking of my poor brother, dead, gone, and I wasn't there to help him. My thoughts go from sadness to severe anger at whoever did this. I scream and scream out loud in my car. How can you do this? How can you take my brother's life? He was such a kind, generous person. He was such a big bear; he was my brother god dammit. Why did you kill him? Oh Sean, Sean, Sean, where are you? Can you see us? Are you okay? Are you in pain? Was it bad? Did you suffer? Oh Sean, why, why, why?

My heart is shattered, falling apart. I have never felt such pain. This is all wrong. The order is wrong, a younger brother is not supposed to die first. My thoughts turn to my father and mother, my heart breaks all over again for them. To lose a child is a parents' worst nightmare, to lose a child to violence must be just unbearable. And Marie, poor little Marie, she is so gentle and sensitive. This is going to break her heart. I lose it again as I think of the pain this is causing Marie. "Why did this have to happen?" I ask. My question of course is unanswered. Why did all the terrible things that have happened this year have to happen? Again, the universe is silent.

I manage somehow to make the drive to dad's without incident. Dad answers the door; his usually jovial face is downcast and solemn. I give him a hug and wish I could take away his pain. I can see he is trying so hard to be brave but I also see confusion on his face. Since my first phone call this morning, Marie, dad and I have been in touch with the RCMP and they are coming over to talk to us within the hour. We still have no explanation as to why they allowed the story to be aired on the news without first informing the family and we still don't fully understand why Sean was killed. When I arrive Marie and her husband Jeff are already there. Soon Tina's son David arrives and we all congregate on the rooftop deck.

This is so alien. This side of the family, other than Bob, Tina's daughter Annabelle who lives in France and our cousin Zara, are all gathered on the rooftop, like we have been for many family celebrations. But something is missing. It's Sean, his huge presence, his 'take me as I am' personality is missing. There is no laughter; there is only shock and pain. Here we sit, this perfectly normal west side family on a perfectly beautiful Vancouver day with a huge frigging hole sitting right in the middle of us.

Conversation is painful but needed. We are awkward, how does one talk about death? How does one understand a violent death? We are all still so new to this, we cannot even imagine the days ahead and how each of us will find our way through this pain.  For now it's a matter of formalities, steps, things that need to be done. My biggest concern right now is my father.  I can see the pain written all over his face and I am terrified that he will have a heart attack from the loss and then as a family our world would truly shatter.

I pull Tina aside for a few moments to ask how dad is doing.  Her response - although honest is hard to take, his heart is broken.  He is hurting so badly, he does not understand any of it, but he is keeping it inside.  I know that Tina will take care of him, they have been together for over twenty years now and she understands him so well. She will hold him when he cries and help him get through this horrible loss.  I wish I could turn back the clock, take away this pain from him, from mum, from Marie.  That is my job.  I am supposed to take care of my family.

I realize that I cannot turn back time, I cannot change what has happened to Sean, but I can make things easier for my family moving forward.  I can take on the responsibility of dealing with everything, I can talk to the RCMP, deal with the funeral, I can do that, and I can at least take that pain away from them.  I also realize this will help me deal with my grief.  My type-A personality will take over.  I will go into autopilot, and I can get this done.

At two o'clock the RCMP arrive.  There are two detectives.  We take them up to the rooftop where we have all gathered.  It is now hot up here, at least thirty degrees in the sun and they are both formally dressed, weapons and all. Quite frankly at this point I don't give a damn. I want to know why no one called my father and had the decency to let him know about his son being killed before it was all over the morning news. It is Marie who lays into them; she has such courage this way. She looks at them and without blinking an eye asks them quite frankly how they could possibly have let the news out without informing Sean's next of kin, Sean's family. She is angry and rightfully so. Of course, they have no answers, at least nothing definitive, their excuse is that Sean's girlfriend arrived on the scene and said she would tell the family. Since when is that considered notifying the next of kin? Marie pushes a bit on this point, but soon she can see this is futile. The two detectives are not budging.

Then comes the questioning. Yes questioning, and not from us, from them. It slowly dawns on me that they are not here to help us. Rather they are here to ask us for details in order to help their investigation. I am quite shocked until I realize that they are only doing this to see if we can be of any help in solving the crime. I look at dad, across the table from me, the pain so obvious all over his face. It is taking all his strength to stop the tears and he has to sit through this interrogation from the RCMP about things he has no clue about.

We spend the next two hours in the blazing heat trying to convince Debra and Lee, the two detectives, that we as a family don't have any insight. It is to them we are looking to for help, for understanding, for some way to put

Sean's murder into perspective.  They are not forthcoming - they are untrusting of us.  We are all relieved when they finally leave.  Dad and I walk them to the door, then we return to the deck where everyone sits in shock.

"Did that just happen?" my stepbrother David asks. "Were they actually interrogating us?  Did they actually think we would know why someone would choose to rob Sean's home and kill him?"

We had all naively assumed they were here to help us, to inform us, to guide us through the process of losing a loved one.  Boy, were we wrong.  Other than letting us know that they would put us in touch with Victims Services, this meeting was all about them gathering information.  Unfortunately for them, in this way, we were all naive.  We didn't have a clue as to why this would have happened.  We were a family locked in shock, sitting here, all of us barely holding on by a string, but the threads drifting around us were somehow managing to hold us all together.

Tina brings up drinks and snacks, and for the first time in a long time the entire family drinks a glass of beer or wine mid-afternoon.  We sit there stunned.

"This is surreal" David says.

We all nod.  It is hard to really say anything - we all feel Sean's presence amongst us.  It is not normal for us as a family to be here, in this spot, without our brother and son.  We eat, we drink and we mourn.  I have never mourned before, I have never seen others mourn before and I don't like it.

It is like this huge painful gap in your chest. Deep in your soul you feel this horrific pain, this regret, anger, sadness, shock and guilt. Guilt because I want to smile and talk about Sean, talk about his silliness and his bravado and his huge personality, but I feel guilty at this sensitive time bringing up the good moments. I even feel guilty talking about any of the memories, perhaps not guilty, but pained, really pained. I look around at my family. All the people I love so much and I see such sadness. I worry about mum.

When Marie called mum this morning she was thankfully not alone. Her sisters had arrived for a visit last week, her sister Stephanie from Germany and her sister Nicki from South Africa. They flew in because of mum's cancer diagnosis and had come to attend her full body CT Scan with her. Also, Marie had called Susan an RCMP officer and friend who lived in the building and had asked her to go upstairs to help explain what had happened to Sean. Marie told me she was shocked by how calm mum was when she told her. I don't really understand it. If I had learned my son had been killed, I know I would have lost my mind. Marie said that Mum however was quiet, quiet as a mouse. We were glad that our aunts Stephanie and Nicki would be there to support mum over the next few days while Marie and I could not. I still did not understand her reaction. It was almost as if she knew, as if she already knew this would happen, like a premonition.

That being said, as I sit here on the rooftop at my father's, my thoughts go to my mother. She and Sean had a special bond. How must she be feeling? Does she really get this? Are her sisters supporting her? I wonder what she must be thinking. How does a mother deal with her son dying? These thoughts are too painful for me to examine. Today mum is also going to get word on the results of her second CT Scan; this will be a heavy day for her indeed.

A few hours later the RCMP come back to the house. It is close to dinnertime now yet we still sit congregated in sorrow on the rooftop deck. The officers look tired as they make their way upstairs and I realize they have been up since the wee hours of the morning working on this. Once again however, they have no further information for us. They are here to get my father's permission to search Sean's house. How odd. We want them to solve this crime, but in order to proceed they need a signed document from dad stating they have the right to search the entire house.

Dad asks again for any information or explanation they might have as to why this happened. There is nothing they can say. I see tears at the edges of my father's eyes and realize he is summoning all his strength here not to cry.

"Where is Sean now? I ask. "I mean, where is his body?"

"He was taken to Royal Columbian Hospital," Debra says.

"Can we see him?" I ask.

"No, the coroner cannot release Sean's body until an

autopsy is done" Debra says. "You need to make arrangements with a funeral home to get him when they are done."

"Okay" I say.

Once again they leave and once again we are left feeling anger and sorrow. I tell dad I'll take care of calling the funeral home and all of that so that he doesn't need to worry about it. Tina decides it's time for us to eat dinner. It is after all almost seven o'clock. We order Indian food and Jeff and David walk up the street to get it.

We set up a huge Indian meal on the deck and hunker down for some comfort food. However today it brings no comfort. There is almost no conversation at the table. We are all thinking of Sean, Sean loved Indian food, and he should be here with us, not lying on a cold slab in a hospital morgue, dead. A tear escapes my eye and makes its way slowly down my cheek. I am too exhausted to brush it away. My mind follows its path as it comes to my chin, hesitates and then makes its long drop to my shirt below. I imagine this is going to be the rest of my life, a long gentle grieving and continual sadness as I miss my brother.

At nine o'clock I decline my father's offer of the spare room, say my goodbyes and drive back home. I am completely numb, on autopilot. I cannot remember anything about the drive except for arriving home exhausted. I give Waldo a quick walk then jump into bed with him. He snuggles up to me and I to him, and then I cry myself to sleep.

I awaken Saturday morning in tears that simply won't stop. Marie calls me. Mum got her CT Scan results yesterday. Mum has lung cancer, in its advanced stages, which has metastasized to the brain, hence all the brain tumours. I am not surprised by this news as mum has smoked almost her entire life. What I do find odd is that she never coughed or had any of the typical symptoms of lung cancer. Mum's prognosis is still four to six months. The doctor wants mum to go in for a biopsy to determine the kind of lung cancer so they can provide some treatment to help alleviate her symptoms. I really don't understand why they want to do this. Mum has already decided she doesn't want any treatment, so why put her through the trouble of the biopsy? Marie and I decide to go and see mum when she has her next doctor's appointment to discuss this.

After making a few calls to funeral homes I make the drive back in to dad's. There is a lot to be done. The RCMP still wish to meet with us and we want some answers. Once again, the family gathers and we go through the day together. Now it's about logistics. When will the autopsy be done? When can we have the memorial? Did Sean want cremation or burial? Was there a will? All these things need to be considered. The RCMP have found a safe in Sean's house, so we are hoping he will have put a will in there. It would be nice if he had written down his wishes.

I call mum late morning. Basil answers the phone and he won't allow me to speak to mum. He says she is resting and that she will call me back later. This is becoming very frustrating, his constant screening of her calls. I decide I'll call her back later rather than waiting for him to pass on a message to mum to call me.

I also get a few phone calls back from funeral homes and decide to book an appointment with George. He seems the most gracious over the phone, and doesn't mind coming out to meet us on a weekend.

The newspapers are now full of coverage over Sean's death and there is lots of speculation going on. The RCMP are quite clear to us and say we are not to believe what is written in the newspapers, that most of what we see there will be untrue and hurtful. We try to keep the papers from dad, or at least warn him first if there is an article, but this will be impossible to do forever. We however continually remind him that what he reads will mostly be untrue and to ask the RCMP if he needs clarification on something.

Later in the afternoon George arrives from the funeral home. We all sit around the dining room table. Dad is in shock. I don't think he ever imagined himself planning his son's funeral.

George is very kind and manages to help us navigate our way through this procedure in a gentle way. George will be going to Royal Columbian Hospital to speak with the coroner about when the body can be released. He will also let me know if I can view the body.

I want to say goodbye to Sean. I want to hold his hand and weep over his body and say goodbye. The rest of the family don't quite understand that, and maybe it's crazy, it's just what I feel is the right thing for me to do.

George warns me that it may not be possible because of the state of the body. He asks if I will accept his judgment call on whether or not this is a good idea, once he has had a chance to see Sean. Reluctantly I agree.

A few of Sean's friends had mentioned that he wanted to be cremated, so we decide to go with that. A simple cremation followed by a small memorial at the house. It is painful watching George ask dad the questions for the paperwork.

"What was Sean's date of birth?"

"What was his address?"

"What was his date of death?"

On and on it goes. I can see how difficult this is for my father and wish it could just be over. All these silly questions like "How big was Sean?" so he can determine if he will fit in a regular sized casket for cremation. Dad, like the rest of us, is still thinking of Sean as alive and well, so to be asked these types of questions seems ridiculous.

I am going to be heading out to Coquitlam today for Rose's soccer tournament. Sean had been invited to watch her play because it is near his house. She has been there since early this morning and has called me twice to find out when I will get there. After George leaves I make my way to her game. I'm not sure how I'm going to handle this. I had spoken to her father earlier and we decided we would not tell Rose and Kory for a couple of days. I wanted to speak to Victims Services to understand the best way to let children know about the loss of a loved one. Sean was very close to both Rose and Kory, so this will be very hard on them.

I cry all the way out to the tournament, so have to sit for a few minutes in the car to pull myself together. I cannot let Rose see anything is amiss.

I manage to catch the last game of the day, and it's an exciting one, as both teams played very well. At the end of the day Rose's team and corresponding parents all meet for dinner at Boston Pizza. I am finding it very difficult to hold it together. I'm not normally this weepy, but the chemotherapy drugs tend to make anyone emotional and the combination of them plus the loss of my brother have brought all my emotions to the forefront.

I excuse myself from the dinner early and go to phone Bob. He has been out of town, but is going to come home early to be with me through this. I tell him that the RCMP will be releasing the scene on Monday night and they have suggested we go there immediately to pack up all of Sean's things and get them into storage. Apparently it's a common occurrence for houses to be vandalized once people know the occupants have died. I need help cleaning out Sean's house. It's big and I'm still sick from chemo and there is no way I can do it alone. Bob says he will be there. He will fly home on Monday and we can go out together. Marie's husband Jeff has also offered to come and help us.

I can see everyone coming out of the restaurant and

heading my way. Rose runs up to me asking if she can hang out with her teammates in one of the rooms until bedtime.

"Sure," I say, "let's just figure out where their room is."

"Mum, she asks, wasn't Uncle Sean coming to watch my game today?"

I feel a stab to my heart. "Yes Rose, he was going to try and make it. Perhaps he got busy with work."

"Maybe he will come out tomorrow," she says.

"Maybe," I reply.

The next day she plays well and forgets about Uncle Sean, as she's too wrapped up in her game. By mid-afternoon I need to go, so I say my goodbyes and make the long drive north to home.

I try reaching mum again when I get home. No luck, Basil still won't put her on the phone. I call Marie. She hasn't spoken to her either. I am a little worried, but her sisters are still there, so if something was really bad, I know they would call me.


Monday, Bob is home finally. I am emotionally exhausted by this point and need his strong shoulders to cry on. We don't have much time before we have to head to meet the RCMP at Sean's. They will be ready to release the scene at six o'clock. We pick up Jeff and make our way out to Coquitlam. It is rush hour so the traffic is very slow and the day is very hot, making it a long ugly drive. We call Debra, the main RCMP officer, at five-thirty. They are not ready for us yet, so we go to a local coffee shop and wait for their call. I want to get in and get it done. We have already organized a moving company to arrive first thing tomorrow morning, and plan on spending the night there packing. The sooner we can get it, the sooner it can be over and the sooner I can get some rest. I am starting to feel the effects of all this stress.

Finally, by six-thirty we are allowed access to the house. Debra warns us that there is a slight possibility the people who broke in before may try again now that they know the RCMP are gone. After a lot of begging and arguing I manage to get them to agree to leave a police cruiser in the driveway as well as have someone drive around through the evening watching the perimeter. The last thing I want is for the three of us to become more victims here.

The RCMP also gave Sean's girlfriend access to the house. I am completely shocked by that. She did not live here so why should she be here tonight. She also gets angry with us for wanting to pack everything up. I try to explain to her that the RCMP have suggested we do this and also as part of dealing with Sean's estate, by law we need to protect his assets until we know what, if any, his wishes were. At this point we haven't found a will, but there may be one in his safety deposit box. I want to start packing immediately but spend the first two and a half hours trying to get her to understand what is going on. Jeff and Bob go out to Home Depot and get a new door — the RCMP bashed in Sean's front door and we cannot exactly sleep here without a front door.

Finally at nine o'clock she leaves. Nine o'clock. This is past my bedtime on a normal night, but since I've been getting chemo, this is far past my bedtime. I am thoroughly exhausted now and have an entire house to get packed. The guys begin to help me by getting boxes made up and I begin wrapping glassware.

Suddenly the motion sensor lights go on in the back yard. We all stop what we are doing and stand very still. "Is there someone here?" we are wondering. We wait. The light turns off and there is no sound in the yard. Probably a cat or something, we think. We continue packing and half an hour later I'm upstairs in the guest bathroom. I have a direct line of sight to the front door and I can swear I see the handle being turned. I keep still and watch intently. Yes, there it goes again. Someone is trying to get in through the front door.

I need to get to Bob and Jeff but if I leave the bathroom and walk down the stairs the person will surely see my shadow and may even take a shot at me. My heart is in my throat. Adrenaline is pounding in my body. How can I tell them? I decide to text Bob and only hope that his cell phone is in his holster, not out on the counter.

"There is someone trying to get in the front door. Don't move. Just tell me where you and Jeff are," I text.

I quickly turn my phone on silent while I wait for his reply.

"We are in the kitchen. I'll go and see what's happening." he replies back.

"No." I manage to quickly text back. "You might get shot like Sean. Please stay there until I can get to you."

"I'll come up," Bob types back.

"No, it is better if we are all on the ground floor," I text.

I cannot get to them and they cannot get to me without either of us having to pass within sight of the front door, which has a frosted glass panel on the side. My hands are shaking as I hold my phone and consider my options. I can only hope Jeff and Bob did a good enough job of securing the door with locks so that the person cannot get in here.

I see the door being visibly pushed inwards, not loudly, there is barely a sound.

My phone display lights up.

"The side lights outside just went on," Bob says.

Okay, that means there is more than one person here. What the hell are we going to do? My heart is pounding. The chemo has my blood pounding double time all over my body and my adrenaline is pumped higher than I have ever felt. I have to get down to Bob and Jeff. "How am I going to do this," I think. I stand there picturing the curved stairwell that I need to navigate in order to get downstairs, picturing how the light from the chandelier might show my presence. The first thing I realize is that I am wearing black. That would show up right away against the cream coloured walls. I need to find something lighter to put on. Fortunately there is a robe hanging behind the bathroom door. I pull that on and wait. There hasn't been much movement at the front door in the last few minutes but I can't risk being seen.

"Bob, I'm coming down slowly. I'm going to hug against the wall furthest from the door and slowly slither down to you guys," I text.

"Okay," he says, "be careful."

I'm not sure why I feel being down with them is better, I just think if we are all together and on the ground floor, perhaps we can make an exit somewhere away from where they are trying to get in. By now we can distinctly hear the sounds of people walking around the outside of the house. The motion lights are no longer going off. They must have removed the bulbs. I have no time to waste. Taking off my black socks I begin my trek down the stairs.

It is only about a fifty-foot walk, but it seems to take forever as I crawl, low to the ground, bathrobe hood covering my head and not looking in the direction of the front door. I slide using my elbows, slowly down the stairwell, like a snake. I slither and slither until I pass the main curve in the stairwell. Now I am out of sight until I get to the bottom, then it is only a quick run, about three feet, until I reach the safety of the kitchen.

I get to the bottom of the stairs, stand, out of sight of the door with my back to the wall. I wait, trying to get my breathing under control. I count one, two, three and I run, quick as a mouse across the gap and into the kitchen. Bob and Jeff are sitting at the table. I am so relieved to see them.

"We need to call the RCMP," Jeff says.

"Yes, where is their card?" I ask.

Bob hands me the card and I make the call. Debra is not in the office. I explain the situation. The officer is aware of us and says he will get Debra right away. Two minutes, which seems like an eternity later, my phone lights up. It's Debra. She can't be here for forty-five minutes.

"What" I say, "that's not good enough. In forty-five minutes we could be dead. These guys are trying to get in and it won't be long before they do."

Debra says she will call the car that is on patrol and get them to the house immediately. "The officer won't come in, but he will make his presence known," she says.

We hear a crash coming from the basement. "He'd better hurry Debra," I say, "I think they are almost inside."

Bob and Jeff and I stay put in the kitchen. I get on the floor and huddle behind the couch. The last thing I want is to die in a spray of bullets. I try to convince them to come and sit down with me, but they won't. They think they are fine at the kitchen table.

We hear a large creaking sound, and then suddenly the windows light up with red and blue flashes. There is a slam from the basement and some rather loud scuffling, then silence. The red and blue lights continue to glow outside like a beacon of safety.

"I think they've been scared off," I say.

We are relieved but still scared. None of us move

until Debra and her crew arrives. We spend almost two hours with them going over the scene again, explaining what we heard and then they decide to take possession of the house again. I'm relieved. I am certainly not going to spend the night here after this experience. We are to meet Debra back here at eight in the morning so we can continue the task of packing up. I'm much happier doing it in broad daylight.

By the time we arrive at dad's house it is one o'clock in the morning. Dad and Tina are away for a couple of days on business, so we can let ourselves in without waking them. I am still buzzing and stressed from the whole evening so decide a glass of wine is in order. Grabbing a bottle from their wine cooler I pour myself a tall glass, pour Bob a beer and we sit down to absorb everything that has just happened to us.

"We could have lost our lives tonight," I say.

"Yes, I don't ever want to go through that again," Bob says.

"You know, when I was younger I always wanted to work for the FBI or the CIA. Now I know I couldn't possibly have done that and lived under this type of life stress on a daily basis. No Siree. One night is enough for me," I say.

It is almost two o'clock before we get to sleep. Tomorrow is going to be a long day.

Sean's memorial is on Friday. It is a quiet affair on the rooftop at dad's. We have some photos displayed of

Sean along with his ashes. I still cannot believe this little box of ashes is all that is left of my brother. I touch it gently as I ask, "Where are you Sean?" "I love you Sean." I look around, the city of Vancouver in all its glory lies before me. "Sean I wish you were here to see this. I wish you weren't dead, this is so unfair." I am so angry at whoever killed him. I want to yell at them and make them hurt just like I hurt. He was our brother dammit. He was a son who was dearly loved. Don't you know what pain you have caused our family?

Mum is one of the first to arrive for the memorial and she looks well. She says she feels fine too, just the occasional headache. That is good I think. Mum has an appointment with her doctor next week. I tell her that Marie and I will come over to go with her. Her sisters are leaving tomorrow after two weeks of visiting so we'd like to be with mum when she goes to the doctor.

By two o'clock everyone is here. There are a few toasts and a few speeches about Sean, but nothing formal. It is all too new, the grief too strong for anyone to really get up and say much. After the guests have left, the family stays until about eight o'clock - we need each other's company, need to feel protected. I spend the night at dad's and, with all the stresses of the past week I am asleep within seconds.

## LIFE MUST GO ON

When someone we love dies, we, the living don't really have much choice other than to go on living. I don't consider this fully living though. A part of me has died. My faith in any higher power has broken. Why would our God or any higher power ever do this, give someone a horrific cancer and then as she is fighting it, kill her brother. It makes absolutely no sense to me, so as a result I am living in a haze, a haze of anger, regret, and disbelief.

I am kept very busy looking after the stuff for Sean's estate and my Oncologist is keeping me very busy with tests and more treatments. I had a repeat MRI. The results came back and the tumour has shrunk significantly. This is really great news. It doesn't mean my treatment plan will be any different, but what it does mean is that the odds of surgery being successful are much greater. I had an Echo Cardio Gram done to check my heart out before starting the next round of chemo (as Herceptin damages the heart), and the results of that are also great.

Speaking of treatment plan, I met with both the Breast Surgeon and the Radiologist on August twenty-seventh, so now I know more about what to expect there. The news was both good and bad.

With regard to my chemotherapy, Sasha has changed my regime and my drug starting this week in order to avoid me having to take massive doses of steroids. I was originally scheduled for four treatments of

Taxotere and Herceptin, both at three week intervals, but that would have meant taking about four times the amount of steroids that I have currently been taking. For me, this would have been a nightmare as I am already struggling with the current steroid dose. So, now I am moving to twelve treatments of weekly Taxol, rather than Taxotere. The idea behind this is that each of the doses will be smaller, so I won't need as many steroids. The challenges are that I'm getting chemo every week, so there won't be the nice "good days" that I have been used to prior to each chemo session. Also, the side affects (which are nasty), are cumulative, so, it apparently gets pretty ugly by about the seventh session.

After the twelve treatments of Taxol/Herceptin, I will get another nine months of Herceptin, (one every three weeks). During this time they will begin the ugly stuff - RADIATION!

I had heard radiation wasn't too bad (when compared to chemo), and that some people's skin will burn and some won't. This is my biggest fear going into radiation. I have pale skin so I am worried about my odds of getting burned. Well, my radiologist assured me not to worry about it. I WILL be burned! Why? Because with IBC, radiation is different. They need to not only kill the cancer inside the breast, but they also need to kill the cancer on the skin. How do they achieve this? By putting a bolus on your skin that acts like an attractant to the radiation and purposely burns the heck out of your skin. Yes you heard right, I'm going to go through twenty-eight treatments of deliberately burning my skin, and not just a small patch. They will treat my entire right side from collarbone to two inches below the breast, from two inches past my midline to all the way under my armpit and around to my back by about four inches. They do this every weekday for twenty-eight days. By the time I'm done, if I haven't lost my mind from the pain of second-degree burns, I will most assuredly be looking like a nicely roasted thanksgiving turkey. So, am I worried about radiation?  Yes I'm now scared to death about it. However, like everything else I have to go through to kill this cancer, I'm going to try and take it one day at a time and hope I make it to the other side.

Once the radiation is done, I get a month's break and then they do the breast surgery. This appears to be easy compared to everything else. In my case what they will do is take skin and tissue from my stomach (yeah free tummy tuck), and re-build my breast. This is good news because not only will I not have an implant, but also I'll have a nice slim tummy, albeit with a huge scar. My surgeon told me not to lose any more weight otherwise there might not be enough there, so I'm going to keep up with my Haagen Dazs routine. Due to the "tummy tuck", the recovery time after the surgery will be two to three months rather than the usual three to four weeks. However she is expecting it to provide far better results than a traditional implant surgery would, both in looks and in keeping the cancer away.

If all goes well I should be healed from radiation and

surgery by June 2013, and off the Herceptin by August - then I hope this nightmare will be over for good. Anyway, now I have an angel looking after me so I hope he gives me the strength I will need over the next few months and keeps cancer away from me for many, many years to come.

All this news is good, but it does nothing to ease the pain from losing my brother. I find if I keep busy working his estate paperwork and going to doctor appointments then I am fine, but when I run across a photograph of him in his belongings, or a note written in his hand, then I break down all over again.

Today I had blood drawn from my port for the first time (they need to draw blood prior to every chemo session and had been using veins up until now). It was pretty painless and once again I was grateful for having the port installed. Tomorrow is the first day of the new chemo drugs Taxol and Herceptin. I'm pretty scared and wish I didn't have to go through this. Bob has been called away to work, which makes me even more nervous. Thankfully my sister has offered to stay with me tomorrow night just in case things get really wacky.

It's chemo day already. My friend Chantal drives me in super early to get my chemo. I slept for only three hours last night so I am already exhausted. Thankfully we have time to have a nice cup of coffee before going into the Chemo Room. As soon as I meet with the nurse I express my concern over this new treatment protocol and ask for Ativan. She says I will be pre-medicated and the Ativan probably won't be needed.

One of the great things about being early for chemo is to get a bed, not a chair (which I find very uncomfortable). I get my port accessed again and some saline dripped in to clear the line and hydrate me. Then they drip in 20mg of Steroids. Within five minutes I am literally climbing the walls. I again ask for Ativan but am told the Benadryl will put me to sleep. The problem with Benadryl is that I get super hyper, like an anxiety attack, when I take small amounts and here they are dripping a large bag worth of Benadryl - party time - NOT for me.

While all this is dripping in I meet with Sasha who confirms everything is going well and that the Radiation prior to Surgery and the Tram replacement is the best option for how my cancer has spread. It will ensure the best success in terms of localized recurrence and the continued Heparin will help prevent recurrence in the blood or bones. He has provided me with the names of two other clinics if I wish to get a second opinion.

After my meeting with him, I go back to my bed and once again request the Ativan. It is finally given to me and I begin to relax. So, they start the Taxol. I guess I am blessed because I have none of the allergic side affect reactions they spoke of. To be honest it was fine, no nasty metallic taste and smell that the Adriamycin (Tiger's Blood) had and I didn't start to feel immediately sick. Taxol took one hour and then they dripped in the Heparin over one and a half hours. Again I had no bad reaction. My body is behaving as it should. Sasha said my cancer has already responded to the A/C treatment, which has more side affects, but when it comes to the Taxol and Herceptin treatments, they are "da bomb" for my kind of cancer. They ought to decimate it.

By the time all is said and done it's two o'clock and I've had a nice little snooze. My sister picks me up and is very kind in that she has offered to come and stay the night with me to watch how I am. Most of the side effects will start tomorrow through Saturday, although I am determined not to get any.

We come home and I sleep for a while, waken, have some yogurt and sleep some more. Then a quick dog walk followed by a lovely healthy dinner - all organic and delicious, thanks Marie. After dinner we watch the movie Amelie. It is really good. Now it's time for bed. All in all, I'm happy for this day and hope to have a good one again tomorrow.

I spoke to an eight year IBC survivor today. I can do eight if not ten or more years. Just takes determination, grit, persistence and courage.

Marie leaves sometime on Friday and my girlfriends begin to arrive to watch over me. I have such a great network of caring friends, always here to help, whether it is to walk Waldo or feed me healthy food. I am well looked after and I feel grateful.

The following week Marie and I meet at the ferry terminal and take the boat over to see mum. First we go to the doctor with her. This meeting did not go well. He kept insisting that mum go and have this biopsy done to determine the type of cancerous cells, yet the reason for this is not to give treatment to cure the cancer, rather to give radiation treatment to limit the effects of the cancer. I can see that mum is not happy by this and is more than a little scared. Regardless, the doctor books the biopsy for the following week.

After this appointment we go and meet with mum's lawyer to make sure her will is up to date and to submit some changes which mum wanted done. By the end of this, mum is tired, so Marie and I take her back home and get her settled. We sit chatting with her on her little balcony for a while. Mum is in good spirits but is talking about which pieces of jewellery she is giving us etc. I don't want to hear any of this. It seems ridiculously too soon. The doctor said four to six months, possibly at the outside even a year, so I don't want to have this conversation. Even though mum's sisters are now gone, she seems to be handling Sean's death well. We don't talk very much about it but I don't see the grief in her eyes that I see in Marie's eyes. She has come to terms with it in some way.

When we leave to take the ferry home, mum is all rested and ready for a quiet evening. I am glad I had met with her doctor to get a better picture of things. I am optimistic that mum will be fine for a long time and that I will have to make a point to spend a lot of time with her over the next little while. I feel grateful I am being given time with mum, whereas Sean was just ripped from my life.

I am so overwhelmed by grief over my brother's death that I cannot wrap my head around anything else. I've never experienced the death of a loved one, so have no idea how to process this. I am angry with God for taking my brother so soon. I wonder why he had to go. I don't understand any of this. All I feel is a huge loss and pain deep in my heart.

My mind keeps asking crazy questions like; did my brother choose to go to save me? If so, I'm really mad at him, that's not fair. Did he go so that there would be someone there looking after our family as we go through the toughest year we've ever had? If so, I'd rather have him here with us so we can talk to him, not gone. I keep asking him to talk to me, to tell me he's okay, that he is happy now, but he's not saying a word. I cannot believe that I'll never see him again. He used to piss me off so much sometimes and now that's all I want is him back so I can get mad at him again.

How does one get over the loss of a loved one? Does one ever stop crying? During the night, I wake up every couple of hours and I miss him. I wake up in the morning and realize again that this is real, not a nightmare, and I miss him. Yesterday I looked through an album from our childhood and it was heartbreaking. He was such a handsome, little boy, all big smiles and big ears, just busting out wanting to be loved. As a little brother he drove me crazy and I was such a pest to him. Now I feel guilty that I didn't love him enough. One of the great blessings that has come out of this loss is that so many people from all over the place have reached out to me and told me how much they loved my brother. They have shared stories with me of his kindness and his generosity and of his love for them. I did not know this side of him. The side that would do anything to help a neighbour or a friend in need, even if it was an inconvenience to him, the side that contributed to World Vision and other charitable organizations, the side that supported people when in crisis and guided them on how to live a better life. I am so glad to hear he was greatly loved and respected by so many people and that he was happy most of the time.

I don't know if this pain will ever go away. I imagine there will come a time when I don't break out in tears at random times throughout the day. Perhaps there will even come a day when I am truly happy again and my memories of him will bring me joy. Until then, I am doing my best to work my way through this and not succumb to the incredible sadness that surrounds me. I am trying to hold my family near and dear and not let anything happen to them and help them to find their own way of healing through this.

"I miss you little brother. Talk to me, will you."

## THE FINAL BLOW

I awake on Tuesday morning to the sound of the telephone ringing. It is Marie. Apparently mum is in the hospital. Basil said that mum didn't make it to her biopsy appointment yesterday. As a matter of fact, she didn't make it out of bed, so by mid-day he and her friend Finn decided to call an ambulance and now mum is in the hospital. Marie and I decide to go over on the next ferry to see what is going on.

We meet at the terminal in the early afternoon; both of us are subdued and worried about mum. We have no idea what to expect when we get there, we saw mum last week and although she was certainly troubled by the tumours in her brain, she seemed well enough overall.

When we arrive at the hospital we are shocked. Mum is completely medicated and out of it. She isn't eating, has only brief moments of recognition and awareness and otherwise just lies there. She looks absolutely frail in the ugly hospital gown and is sweating due to the sunshine streaming into her south-facing window. She is sharing a room with three other women patients. One has Alzheimer's and spends her time sadly wandering around the room.

The nurses are kind, but it's not like family. Marie and I spend the afternoon with mum, trying to interest her in food, trying to keep her cool and waiting to find out from her doctor what is going on. It is after five before we finally get to see him. He doesn't have any real answers for us. All he can say is that this is a result of the cancer and all he can do for her is keep her comfortable. I am angry with this, it's as if he's not willing to try anything, but perhaps those are mums wishes. It just seems too soon. I ask if she is dying, he simply shrugs his shoulders and says probably. Marie and I are devastated. We have just lost Sean; I don't think we can handle losing our mother now as well. We go back and sit beside her bed, gently holding her hands, placing cold face cloths on her hot forehead and looking across at each other with worry and pain in our eyes.

At eight o'clock Bob and Jeff arrive. Marie and I are tired and hungry, so after the men have a brief visit with mum we say goodnight and go to get something to eat. After dinner, Bob and I get a room at a local motel. Neither of us can sleep and it is long past one in the morning before we finally turn in. The next day we are up early and all meet up at the hospital again.

Through the evening they have changed one of the patients in the room and now the bed next to mum's has a rather large man with type two diabetes who was brought in through emergency last night. He spends most of his time coughing and hacking loudly and every time he does, mum awakens in concern. Mum would be mortified to know a man is sharing a hospital room with her, she is very conservative and this would put her over the edge.

There has been no change in her condition overnight, but during the day the four of us manage to get her interested in Haagen Dazs and apple juice. This is a huge improvement over yesterday. She manages to consume at least four small hospital sized juice containers during the day.

We decide to call mum's sister Stephanie in Germany to let her know what is happening and to ask her if she can come back. It has barely been two weeks since she left, but it is serious enough now that she should come back if she can. Fortunately mum's other sister Nicki hasn't made the return trip back to South Africa and is still in Germany. They make the decision to book a flight out on Friday and I call to see if the B&B they stayed in last time is available. We book a large suite for Stephanie and Nicki and a room for both Marie and I. Thankfully no more cheap motel.

Today at the hospital is relatively uneventful. Mum is in and out of consciousness. We do our best to try to keep her cool in the heat and to keep her mouth fresh and her skin moisturized. Being in a hospital bed without proper food and without the ability to get up and move around is no picnic, but thankfully the pain medications for the tumours are also treating some of the back and leg pain she must be feeling.

Looking after mum is difficult - every time I sit by her bedside I cry. I try not to show her my tears because I am not sure if she knows she is dying. I also hope that maybe she is not dying, that maybe she will get better after some days rest here. When I am not with Marie beside mum's bed I am numb. It is as if I am on autopilot, my thoughts and my feelings are not connecting, and I don't feel like I am living in reality. Maybe this is the way we humans cope with overwhelming grief and pain. I'm not certain; I just notice that I feel I've been anesthetized.

The following morning Bob and I have to be up very early. It is chemo day. We take the early morning commuter ferry to North Vancouver and before I can fully wake up I am sitting in a bed at the hospital waiting for my treatment. Suddenly because I am away from mum and Marie I cannot stay strong anymore. I just lie here sobbing. Once my port has been accessed and the chemo started, I curl up into a little ball under the blankets and let the medications take me off to sleep.

Five hours later Bob drives me back to the ferry and waits with me for the ferry to come. I am a walk-on passenger and Marie is picking me up on the other side. I sleep most of the ferry ride and am a bit of a zombie when Marie gets me, but I'll get through it.

Mum has not improved at all today. As a matter of fact she has deteriorated and by the time I get to the hospital she is completely non-responsive. Marie and I stay for a short visit, then go to eat and back to the B&B. Mum's sisters will arrive tomorrow. I just hope they get here in time.

Friday is much the same. We spend the day by mum's bedside, but she has not improved. Through the evening her Alzheimer's neighbour stole her robe and is now wearing it, and another much larger man has replaced the male patient. We manage to have some brief moments of humour with mum, one of the funniest was when the man decided he needed to go to the toilet, and instead of walking the three feet to the toilet in the room, he walked two feet to the portable toilet and proceeded to stink up the entire room. It was so bad you could smell it in the hallway. Anyway, mum has always been very polite and well mannered, and here she was lying in her stupor when the pungent odour reached her nostrils. Her eyes popped wide open and she said quite loudly "I didn't fart, that wasn't me." Marie and I giggled madly at that and only hoped the man was deaf as well as stinky and did not hear that.

Finally after a long day Auntie Stephanie and Auntie Nicki arrive with Bob who had met them at the airport. Marie and I are exhausted and so relieved to see them. I can tell that they are very shocked by mum's condition, especially considering how well she was not two weeks ago. Mum does manage to wake up and acknowledge their presence, but her energy is short lived and soon she is drifting again.

We discuss bringing mum home to care for her there and two days later after much pestering of her doctor and many conversations with palliative care, we are given permission to do so. The palliative care people are fabulous, they arrange for a hospital bed to be set up in mum's bedroom, and arrange for a once daily nursing visit and a once daily homecare visit. Marie and I put mum's pillow and her nice fresh quilt on her bed to make it seem a little homier.   The ambulance arrives at around four o'clock with mum and shortly afterwards Patricia from palliative care arrives.  She is amazing.  She explains that mum has a pain patch on her chest that will look after the balance of the pain, but that we need to top her up every four hours or so, as needed, with a shot in through a butterfly in her arm.  We also need to give her Decadron twice a day to help alleviate the swelling in her brain.  In the evening at about nine o'clock mum gets a sleeping pill to help her sleep as the Decadron is a stimulant.  Patricia ensures that we realize this is twenty-four hour care and asks us if we think we are capable of doing this. Fortunately there are four of us, so we assure her we will take turns, two of us every second night, giving each team a break.  Patricia says that the homecare attendant will be by later to show us how to change mum and turn her and keep her comfortable in her bed.  They will do the bathing, so we don't need to be concerned with that at this time.

Once mum is settled and Patricia leaves we go out into the kitchen to speak with Basil and all hell breaks loose.  He is very upset that we have brought mum home from the hospital, even though he knows very well that is her wish.  We try to explain to him that he doesn't need to do anything, that we four will be here twenty-four hours a day.  We also try to help him understand that this is much easier for him too.  He no longer has to make the long trek to the hospital to see mum, he will have his meals prepared for him and he won't be alone during this difficult time.  It doesn't matter what we say.  We could speak until we were blue in the face, as he is having none of it and is adamant we have made the wrong decision and that mum should go back to the hospital. This is very upsetting for all of us and we eventually leave him to his own devices and go back to sit with mum.

So begins the most difficult two and a half weeks of my life. I had no idea how challenging it is to care for someone you love, especially if you know they are not getting better, they are dying and you are simply there to help ease the process for them. My aunts and my sister have an extra load because once a week I have to go to the city for chemo which means I will be a bit of an emotional mess for the next few days afterwards.

There are days when mum is coherent and I tell her how much I love her and I sit and cry and she asks me "Why are you crying Michelle?"

"I don't know mum," I say. How can I tell her it is because she is dying and I am sad? How can I say that to her?

Sometimes when I come and sit beside her she smiles, takes my hand and says "My little one, my sweet little one". That breaks my heart. Mum always called me her "little one" and I always want to be her little one. I don't want her to die, I love her and I need her. Her grandchildren need her, we all need her. On some days she looks so beautiful and peaceful lying there. My mother is a very beautiful woman and even in dying she is gorgeous. We keep her hair brushed and her sister Stephanie religiously applies mum's favourite face creams every day.  Sandy, mum's hairdresser even comes and gives mum a nice hair wash.

The first week we see an improvement in mum's condition, so I am hopeful.  On one particular morning I walk out into the kitchen to get some tea and Basil asks how mum is doing.

"She is doing very well," I say, "she may even be able to get to the toilet by herself next week."

"Don't be stupid Michelle," Basil says.  "Your mother is not getting any better.  She's never getting out of that bed, how can you say something so stupid?"

I am hurt and I am angry.  I am so sick and tired of his nasty behavior and his using the fact that he is an old man as an excuse, I lash out.  "Why would you say that? Mum can get better.  How can you tell me she is never getting out of bed again?  That's a terrible thing to say."

Basil does not care, he continues on as if he hasn't heard me.  I leave the room in frustration.  I hope mum didn't hear any of that.

On another day mum is hallucinating about airplanes flying overhead.  She points to them and says they are from Afghanistan.  This is not the first time she has done this.  When she was in the hospital she also saw airplanes from Afghanistan overhead.  I wonder if it is from growing up in Germany during the war, and whether she is imagining these airplanes and relating them to the most recent war, the one in Afghanistan.

Often mum sees someone in the corner of the room. We never know who it is, but she sees someone and it's very strange to watch, almost eerie.

The children come to visit and it is bittersweet. Mum recognizes them right away and gives them hugs and asks how they are doing, and then she becomes quiet and the children, especially Rose, become sad. When they leave an hour later she says sadly, "Mum this will be the last time I see Granny won't it?"

"Yes," I say, giving her a hug "yes it will be. I feel so bad for my children. They have a mother with cancer, their uncle has just been killed and now their Granny is dying. How much can one family bear?"

The week following the children's visit, mum goes downhill fast. Her moments of lucidity are short and she is asleep most of the time now. Today we had a funny moment. I was sitting holding mum's hand when I got a hot flash and had to quickly remove a layer of clothing and my toque. Unbeknownst to me, my toque had left deep grooves in my baldhead and mum looked at me in surprise and then started laughing. She rubbed my head gently, smiling at me. I will never forget that moment, one of the last coherent ones, and I am saddened that one of the last memories my mother had of me was when I was bald. I know it's silly, but I wanted her to be here to see my hair grow back. I wanted her to be here for so much more.

Every morning the nurse visits and gives us a prognosis. It is hard having these conversations, hard sitting here on what equates to deathwatch. I am still hoping for a miracle, that somehow mum will pull through and perk up and start eating again. She hasn't had much to eat in the last few days and is starting to decrease her water intake as well. This makes it very difficult for us to give her the medication she needs. Patricia tells us that at this point the medication doesn't really matter, that mum doesn't notice things anymore. I'm not so sure about this. So we try for a few more days to give her the Decadron and her sleeping pill, but eventually we give up. Mum says she is "checking out". I guess that is her way of saying it's over. I guess she must know.

By the end of September we are all becoming quite exhausted, both emotionally and physically. Mum has been a trouper and is still hanging in with us, but unfortunately has slid down beyond any return, so really we are just easing her way. Every second night Marie and I stay with mum and every other night we let the Aunts stay and we sleep at the B&B a block away. We are tired and we are sad. We walk without smiling, we have no more joy, and it is all dark now. It has been a month since Sean died and my soul feels ripped out and ripped off.


It is Sunday September thirtieth. Mum has not been conscious for most of the day today. Her breathing has also started to become much heavier, more laboured. Nicki and I manage to go out for a glass of wine near the end of the day. We sit in the fall sunshine down by the ocean. The spot is lovely and it is such a beautiful early evening, which makes me even sadder. Mum will never get to enjoy this again. She will never see sunsets again and never awaken to the sound of birds outside her bedroom window. How can life just be taken away like this?

After a while we head back up to the house. Marie and I are staying tonight so around nine o'clock we say goodnight to the Aunts. I manage to stay up late with Marie, however at around one in the morning I start drifting off. Marie is sitting in mum's old bed watching Netflix and I'm sleeping in the blow up mattress at the foot of the bed. This is where I slept when I would spend the night with mum after my work visits to the area, earlier this year. It seems so long ago now. I drift off and wake up, hear mum's breathing and drift off again. At some point in my sleep I am conscious of the sound of mum's breathing changing, I open one eye and see Marie sitting beside her bed, I am tired, I cannot stay awake, and I drift back to sleep. Mum's breathing has become very loud now, so for some reason that seems to me to mean everything is okay. I am drifting in and out, listening to her breathing, then I'm dreaming, then listening, then dreaming. Suddenly Marie shakes me.

"She is gone. Mum is gone," she says.

I sit up in shock. "No? When?" I ask.

"Just now," she says.

"I don't understand, what happened?" I ask

"She just stopped breathing, it looked hard, like she was struggling a little bit, and then she just stopped breathing." Marie says.

I go to mum's bedside and take her hand. Already it is colder, changed somehow. "Mummy, mummy, mummy" I quietly weep next to her, holding her hand. Her eyes are open, Marie tries to close them gently but they don't want to close. I keep looking for mummy, looking for her spirit around me or in the room, but I don't feel her anymore.

We sit for a few minutes with her and then call the Aunts. It is almost six in the morning now, we won't wake Basil to tell him, rather we will let him know as soon as he awakes. The Aunts arrive within minutes and we hug each other, holding on for dear life. Stephanie sits by mum and talks to her, stroking her beautiful face and whispering little secrets to her. I sit at mum's desk in shock. Why did I think it would be easier this way? Easier to spend time accepting mums death and be ready for it when it comes in comparison to the way we lost Sean. I have no idea; I just know I was mistaken. There is nothing easy about this

By British Columbia law we have to wait an hour before we can call the funeral home, and then they take a few hours to get here. During this time mums' eyes have closed gently on their own, but her essence is gone. Her skin looks as cold and pale as porcelain. We have to remove her jewellery before they arrive and I am afraid to hurt her when I do this - how silly of me to think that.

Marie gets something nice out for mum to wear for her ride to the funeral home and makes sure she is comfortable.

At eight o'clock Basil wakes up so we give him some private time with mum. He has been in a few times each day to spend time with her and he says that he said his goodbyes days ago, so doesn't spend very long with her now. I can see that he is upset and feel badly for him despite his meanness.

Finally the funeral home attendants arrive. They are kind and efficient. They suggest we leave the room while they do the transfer, and we do so gladly. I don't think any of us want to watch mum being transferred to their stretcher and taken away. This would be too much. A few minutes later they come to let us know they are finished. We walk back into mum's room, a morbid group, heads hung low. The room is empty now. Just like that, mum is gone. Gone where? I don't know. Is she with Sean? Did he help guide her to the other side? Or is that just bullshit, just some fantasy we make up to make ourselves feel better.


We spend the next few days making arrangements, meeting with the funeral director, the lawyer, and the place where we will have the memorial. Haven't we just done all this not so long ago? Marie and I go through mum's phone book notifying her friends and asking them to notify everyone so we don't miss anyone. The memorial will be on Friday. It will be a quiet tea by the ocean. In the morning we, the family, will gather to lay mum's ashes to rest in a spot that she and Basil had already chosen years ago, then we will go on to the public tea.

Bob arrives and spends these last days with us, and then he and I head home. Marie follows shortly afterwards and the Aunts stay on to look after Basil.

When I arrive home I am still in shock and once again my amazing network of friends reaches out to support me. I go over to Michele's for tea and cry in her arms. It has been years since I've allowed myself to cry in a friend's arms. It feels good. I am grateful for her love.

Today is Thursday, chemo day again. I'm feeling especially sad today. I am pretty sure it's a combination of the chemicals that are injected into me, the pain killers and the personal stress that I am under that is contributing to my overall sense of sadness and loss.

Bob is playing some beautiful music downstairs on his guitar and it makes me sad when I hear it because I realize that two very special people in my life will never hear music again. They will never wake up to see a sunrise again or smell the fresh morning air. Seeing the waves washing against the shore on Davis Bay on Tuesday tore my heart out.

Mum and I used to walk the pier there and go for dinner at Sirens. Now she will never be able to do that again. I cannot believe that in two short months God has chosen to take away two of my family members. This is so unfair. I am not ready for this. I know it's selfish, but I need mum to help me get well and hold my hand through chemo, radiation and surgery. I feel terrible that her last memories of me were when I was sick and bald. I didn't want mum to leave worried about me. I wanted to be healthy. I can't believe I'll never see mum or Sean ever again.

I fall back asleep, but even my dreams are haunting. It's not long before I am awake again sobbing into my pillow. This is how it goes through most of the night. On Friday morning when we leave to catch the ferry for mum's memorial, I am exhausted.

We all meet at the cemetery. The children are here and Basil and his children, and the aunts and Marie, Jeff, Bob and I. We are a sad little group. I do not know quite what to say as we all stand there around mum's little spot in the ground. Somehow I manage to get some words out, but when it comes time to lay her ashes in the ground I cannot do it. Thankfully mum's sister Stephanie was able to take over and gently laid mum's ashes into the hole, then each person takes a turn to put some dirt on top. Finally a rose bush is planted to mark the spot. It all goes so quickly and soon it is time to go. I don't want to go. I don't want to leave mum here. She is not supposed to be in the ground. She is supposed to be with us. With great sadness and a heavy heart I walk away. "Goodbye mummy," I think as I go. "I love you."

The memorial is lovely.  Lots of people come to show their respects.  Finn makes a nice speech and then everyone mills around looking at photographs of mum or chatting with one another.  Funerals are so odd I think.  I hate them and I don't want to go to another one for a long, long time.

After I got home this evening I felt a desire to express my sadness in a poem.

<u>*Goodbye Mummy*</u>

*Today I laid my mother to rest.*
*Just as the sun was beginning it's descent to the west.*
*I stood quite still, overcome with grief.*
*Shocked and in complete disbelief.*
*Holding onto her ashes I thought to myself, how can my mother be gone?*
*Her life was not meant to be over, don't you see, this is all wrong.*

*She was so kind and gentle, so loving and true.*
*Always cheering me up, when I was feeling blue.*
*As I grew older she was constantly there.*
*A silent presence who really cared.*
*This can't be happening, I scream inside,*
*I still need her; she is my beautiful life guide.*

*No one is listening don't they see.*
*This is not how it was supposed to be.*

*I didn't want my mother to die, not yet, not now.*
*We were not finished, my mother and I.*
*We had dreams and plans and things to do.*
*Now they are dead, gone with you.*

*Losing you has left a big hole in my heart.*
*You were my Mummy, my special one.*
*You loved me and cared for me and held me when I cried.*
*My life has changed now that you have died.*
*I shall miss you forever, every night and every day.*
*My life is not the same now that you have gone away.*

*Goodbye Mummy, God speed.*
*Fly with the angels and pay us no heed.*
*I hope you are happy and in no more pain.*
*I hope you are running in meadows and laughing again.*
*It may not be soon, but I'll see you again one day.*
*We'll laugh and we'll cry and together we'll play.*

# I AM DEAD

Since Sean and mum have died, both quickly, tragically and unexpectedly in the last two months, I have been barely living. I feel as if half of my entire life has just been ripped away from me and it can never come back. There were desperate days where I just didn't want to go on, I missed them both so much and could not imagine a life without them. I have also lost all my faith in life and in death. I guess you could say I'm like the little girl who believed in Santa and fairies and then one day found out that Santa didn't exist and fairies aren't real either. I feel as if my love of life "my naiveté" has been stripped from me like a thick skin, the rose coloured glasses smashed in the process. Now all I see is the sufferings of life followed by death, followed by nothing. It's over! The end! Nothing more exists, so why do we bother to be here in the first place?

To come back out from this headspace is pretty hard to do. I am now angry and don't want to play at this silly game of life anymore. From what I have seen of death and from what I've read, there is nothing after death. Sean and mum didn't reunite in each other's arms with joy. He wasn't there waiting for her because there is no there, it's just nothing, big dead blank! We all like to think lovely stories about when we die we will meet up with those we loved and hold them again, and will we communicate in subtle ways with those left behind to guide them to be better people.  No, it's all just a hopeful fantasy, a way for those of us still living to prepare ourselves mentally for dying, and for those who lost loved ones, to make the passing of the loved one easier on the ones left behind. When we die, when our body stops pumping blood, breathing and pulsing, then that's it.  We slowly become cold and hard and our colour seeps out of our skin.  We look like frozen zombies, we don't feel human anymore because we aren't.  All that is left is a bunch of cells that were once living and have now been shut down.  There is no love left there, no kindness, no joy, just a used body. THE END.

So, as I go through each day, each moment, hoping each will be a little better than the last I realize I'm stuck. I am cynical and angry about life, about what a stupid game it is and that we are all suckered into it for what?  To grow up, get jobs, become model citizens, have families, grow old and one day we just die.  All we did, all we had was pointless, it meant nothing, we're dead.  When I'm dead, I'm not going to care about the nice sheets I had on my bed, or the excellent coffee maker I bought, or my car that I love, or the gas fireplaces that keep the house warm in the winter.  Really I'm not going to care and neither is anyone else, so why do all this in the first place?  Is it because we feel we have to do something, we have to live civilized lives with all the trappings?  We have to be seen in the right clothes with an iPhone (not Android or Blackberry), with cool boots and drive a cool car.  Our kids must go to the best schools and do well in school and achieve, achieve, achieve, for what? They too will die and what is it all for?

This earth is over-populated already, so why are we still able to have children? Why don't we stop birthing for a while, let the populations drop and then when we're back to a more manageable size, we can procreate again but in controlled amounts. I still don't see our purpose, I mean look, even ants and bees have a purpose. They are born, they collect food to feed the queen, they collect stuff to build the ant nest or beehive, and then in time they die. However they did not live without a purpose. Their purpose is clear, to keep the queen alive so that the bees may continue to live so they can spread the pollen for the flowers. Job well done. Humans, we're born, we're cute for a while, and then we cause our parents and possibly teachers and others all kinds of grief. We become workers in the system so we can bring home a paycheque to spend on "things". We drink too much, we commit crimes, we do drugs, we damage others, the earth, the animals and then we die. The good ones when they die leave others grieving (how kind), and the others die without mention or memory - so really what's the point here?

When I think of my own personal hell that I've lived these last five months I don't see much purpose in a lot of it anymore. If this cancer doesn't go away completely, or if it comes back within three years, which it has more than a sixty percent chance of doing, then I have a difficult decision to make. Having gone through chemo and knowing what "life" it sucks out of you, I'm not willing to do that again. I mean why live if you have no quality of life. However on the flip side, having just lost my mummy and fully understanding the pain and heartbreak that comes from losing ones mum, I feel a strong responsibility not to do that to my children. They are too young to lose a mum, it would change their lives forever (I'm sure this year has already done a bit of that to them), but on top of it all to lose their mother would be too much. So I feel an obligation to fight to stay alive for them, and for Bob and the rest of my family because they love me. However, if it came back, my choice would be to not poison myself again and make my life a living hell again. My choice would be to live the last few months as best I can by doing all the things on my bucket list and dying with smiles and memories and loved ones who will remember all the great times we had together. I'm not going to any heaven or beautiful place to run and play with my mum after this, so I'm not saving any of myself for that. I want to lie there dying knowing that I've managed to take Bob, Rose and Kory back to Africa, my home; that I've managed to take them to Germany to show them all the wonderful places I spent my childhood Christmases. I want to go to Disneyland with Kory and Rose, to go camping again with them, to go snorkeling in the South Pacific with them by my side, to go out for nice family dinners after our day trips and talk like old friends for hours so that I can learn all about them and their lives and their dreams and their wishes. I want to die knowing that I truly knew them and they truly knew me so that when I am nothing but ashes, in their hearts and minds I'll still exist as the mother who said she was Tinkerbell, who raced around the house doing somersaults just for fun, who did crazy things with them and rode all the rides with them and loved them and read to them and cuddled them all the time.

So, although when I'm gone, there will be no second world, or after life for me, I hope I will live on in the hearts and minds of my loved ones. I would want them not to be sad and think of my last few years as being sick and down with cancer treatments. Rather I want them to remember them as being a blast. I want them to remember that we travelled the world together, we ate crazy food together, we saw amazing things together, but mostly we loved and we laughed. That will be my legacy, my gift. Now if only I can find a way to make this happen.

In the meantime being the stubborn fighter that I am, I know I have to get back on the horse and get back on with the job of living. The original Michelle is gone, dead and gone. I'm not sure who this new person will be but I need to find out, I need to give myself a kick in the butt and start working on it.

Now, I'm not sure if making this decision is my way of saying to the universe, listen, you can't hit me with anything else because I'm now on the road back up or if I think I am really ready to start on the road back up.

However, today I took a small step. A few days ago I registered for a Women's Leadership Workshop that took place today. In the past I would have attended this type of an event with the goal being to improve my business and my career. This time, I chose to go for two reasons, one, I was intrigued by one of the topics and two; I wanted to try to "get back out into the world". I mean I do have to go back to work one day and continue to contribute to society.

Since being ill and losing mum and Sean I have been avoiding people. At first, being ill kept me home because I have been too sick to work or do much other than sleep and recover from chemo. Then, since their deaths, I have been too fragile to go out. I would break down at the smallest show of kindness from anyone, so to avoid this I've just stayed away from people.

Today was a big step for me and it started quite well. I managed to get through the registration, say hello to a few people I knew and find myself a spot at a table without doing anything out of the ordinary. Then when the sessions began, the trouble began. You see the first session was about finding and living your passions. This was something I came for, something I wanted to do; yet how can I find my passions when my soul is broken? How can I think of momentum, moving forward when I'm still stuck in pain and loss and grieving? This was the first time in my life I realized I'm not one of those dolls that just bounce back up when you push them down. I've always been able to do that, but now it's going to take more than a bounce or momentum to get me back up. I can see this is going to be a slow, step-by-step process. There will be days where I can make steps forward, and there will also be days where my grief, or the chemo or my exhaustion will stop me or even pull me back down a notch. Not only am I going to have to show myself patience as I go through this process, but I'm also going to have to learn who I've become.

I am certainly not the woman I was before. I don't even know who I am now. I have some idea of what is important to me and an inkling of how I'd like to live my life moving forward, but it is by no means a clear picture. I know that I want to spend more time with my family than ever before, although how that looks I don't know. I know that I want to show my children and my husband the world and enjoy new experiences with them, but how I'm going to achieve that, I have no idea.

So to think I could just rush back into life and "get back on the horse" was a big mistake. This recovery is going to take time. I have the emotional recovery to go through, and then when I am done with chemo, radiation and surgery I will have the physical recovery to get through. I don't know who will emerge at the end, have no idea what my life or I will be like then, so it's almost like giving birth to a new being. Just like nurturing your body during pregnancy, I'm going to have to nurture my body, my heart and my soul over the next few months so that I can bring forth a stronger, happier more enlightened version of the person I was, someone who can continue my journey in this world with more faith and love and passion than I ever could.

## HEALING

October is finally over and we are in the thick of fall. As I look outside my window I see the wind playing with the few remaining leaves on our maple tree. Soon winter will be here. Not my favourite time of year and this one will be especially sad. I am still in weekly chemotherapy, which ends on the twenty-second of November. I cannot wait for that. I am having difficultly getting beyond my grief and have realized I need some help with this. A girlfriend suggested I check out The Callanish Retreat. It is a special retreat for cancer patients to come, spend time being pampered with massages, great food as well as learning to come to terms with death. I called them to ask if I would be able to come even if some of my "coming to terms with death" would be learning to accept my loss of mum and Sean. They were very encouraging, so I am looking forward to attending the retreat next week.

Kory and Rose are slowly starting to come around, particularly Rose who was really traumatized over her Uncle's death. We don't spend a lot of time talking about Sean or mum, but then again I don't avoid the subject either. Bob has been taking care of me as usual and will be going up north to visit his family when I go to my retreat. I think the break will be good for him too.

We human beings are amazing creatures, I think, as I watch the wind in the trees. We take a beating and keep on going, such resilience, and such spirit. It really is a wonder.

I have just finished my week at the Callanish Retreat and am completely blown away. I had no idea what to expect when I came here, I just knew that I had a lot of pain, grief, anger, disappointment and fear residing within me and wanted to find a way through that.

Being here has allowed me to explore everything in a safe and loving environment. It has helped me come to terms with the loss of my mother and Sean, and the possibility that I may not live as long a life as I may have wished. I have shed more tears here than I ever thought possible, but as I did, the layers of pain and disappointment fell away. Sometimes, they fell away only to reveal a deeper hidden fear that I was not aware of, and sometimes they fell away leaving me feeling stronger and more optimistic.

I miss my mother and brother terribly, but I'm starting to accept that they have moved on to another realm. I spent a lot of time trying to be with Sean at his moment of death because I feel so sorry that I could not help him then and that he was so alone. I wanted to go back as a little angel and be with him and tell him that everything was going to be okay, and to stop his pain, his sadness, his sorrow and his fear. I wanted to tell him that I loved him and that I was sorry that I was so nasty to him when I was a little girl. I wanted to hold his heart and his little hand and guide him to the other side with love and caring. I think working with everyone here helped me to do that and to accept that he has gone but that he is still with me in my heart.

Working through mummy's death was very hard for me; I still struggle with her being gone and keep wanting to share my days with her. I am so sad that she could not live a longer life with us and laugh and love some more. I thought a lot about the nights I would spend with her when I was working on the coast, about sitting up until ten o'clock watching HGTV and then waking her up at six in the morning by tickling her foot under her quilt. I understand that it was her time and am glad that she went in peace and I'm slowly coming to feel a sense of peace and acceptance around it myself. I may not be able to speak with her directly again, but I am beginning to have daily conversations with her like I did when she was alive and that helps me feel connected to her.

Facing the fact that I have cancer and may die sooner than I would like was relatively easy until I thought about my children. Then this incredible anger surfaced. I cannot possibly abandon these two lovely beings that I brought into this world, I absolutely refuse to do that, not until they are ready to be on their own in life. I have faced my own death and am okay with that, but I'm not okay with that happening anytime in the next ten years. So I have my work cut out for me. I will fight this disease every step of the way and with everything I have to get rid of it and to stop it from coming back. I will raise my children into loving, happy, responsible adults no matter what it takes. When my time comes, I'll be ready for it. I am no longer afraid of what lies on the other side, I have just put my foot down and will not allow it to come to me while my children still need me.

So, although I was only on retreat for a week, I feel I have come a very long way. I spent a week being cared for by a group of Angels who devote their lives to bringing peace, understanding and acceptance to those who are suffering from cancer. They fed my heart with love, fed my mind with ideas and information around living for all that is possible, and they fed my body with the most delicious food I have ever tasted.

The biggest blessing I have come away with is to have bonded with a loving community of individuals who are walking a similar path and for whom I now feel such love and compassion. We are all here for each other and understand without judgment how profoundly a diagnosis of cancer affects our lives. These are the people to whom I can turn during those dark days and I also know that I will be here for them to help pick them up when life becomes too much. We each have our families and support people outside of this group, and without them we would be lost, however there is nothing quite like connecting with someone who is experiencing or has experienced the same pain, anxiety and fear.

Life is insanely unfair and unpredictable. However in all of that unpredictability it somehow manages to bring us joy, love and fulfillment. My time at the Callanish

Retreat brought me all of that and more and I am truly grateful for the experience.

## THE LAST UGLY CHEMO SESSION

This coming Thursday I will pass a very important milestone in my treatment and although I am thrilled to be doing so, I am also saddened by news of my friends from the Callanish Retreat. My prayers and thoughts go out to them as they are struggling with terrible setbacks and have to once again get on the cancer roller coaster not knowing what is in store for them. My heart aches for all of them.

My progress in this journey, although it seems like forever to me, is actually still in the beginning stages. I haven't yet reached the stage where I am "Cancer Free", so fortunately haven't had to deal with the cancer coming-back news. If you think getting cancer is hard, then imagine how devastated one must feel when after months and months of fighting with all you've got, finally feeling that you are over it, you get the news that it is back. Your world must just come crashing down around you. I can almost feel that terrible sense of loss deep in your heart as you fall to your knees sobbing. This awful gut wrenching feeling is something I must avoid at all costs, so I will battle this slimy enemy until he is exhausted and gives up altogether.

This Thursday is my last Taxol treatment. Yeah, three evil chemotherapy treatment regimes will be done, completely gone, and hopefully I will never do have to do them again. I am amazed at how I managed to make it through them. I remember the days when I was so ill I thought I was going to die, or would rather have died than go for another chemo session. I remember having the ambulance called because I could not breathe, and then when they got here, they couldn't find a pulse - I remember asking them "Please don't let me die". Ah the power of the human spirit, here I was so sick I wanted to die, yet begging the ambulance attendant not to let me die on the way to the hospital. I remember dry heaving on the toilet and ending up in tears on the bathroom floor for hours. I was so angry, so lost, so scared. I felt so guilty for having cancer, I felt I had failed my family and everyone else. I was terrified before each chemo session, but somehow managed to wake up, sing my way through my shower and show up at the hospital all smiles and ready to go. I slept through most treatments because I was too afraid to look around and realize where I was. I was one of the dying, I was in a room being given one of the worst treatments on earth for one of the worst diseases on earth, and I was twenty plus years younger than most of the other patients. I didn't want to know this. So I asked for an Ativan each time and closed my eyes and drifted off while silently praying for all this to go away. Every time I woke up it was to the beautiful blue eyes of my loving husband who never left my side (other than to go and get my meds while I slept). He has been with me every step of the way. He has held me when I cried, helped me to walk when the pain was too much, kept me fed with delicious meals, even if I couldn't eat them all, cheered me up when I didn't feel like getting out of bed for days and always, always been there for me. When he had to go away to work, then my amazing friends appeared, bringing soups, casseroles, fruit, vegetables and lots of loving kindness. My children were looked after, my dog was walked, my house was taken care of and my spirits were cheered up. I am so grateful to Bob and everyone who helped me get through this terrible time; there is no possible way I could have done this alone.

I am going to make sure I celebrate this last Taxol treatment in style. I am going to bring champagne to the chemo ward and ask my friends to join me in a toast. I cannot think of a better way to say bye bye to Nasty Chemo for GOOD!

Next up, Herceptin continues. Yes, I'm not quite done with chemo; I still have to complete my Herceptin cycle, which will take me until August 2013. It's only every three weeks though, and if my heart takes it easy and doesn't get too damaged, then things should all progress well.

Lucky for me, I do have a mini break in December. You see, after hitting me with the hard chemo for six months or so, I now get a month off (except for the Herceptin), to recover before they begin radiation in January. R A D I A T I O N ........... Radiation is the next test in my battle for domination. I can do it though, I'm a fighter, and I can handle six weeks of being hit with radioactive rays. You bet I can. I'll have Bob with me every day and my family has offered for me to stay with them if the drive becomes too much during the last few weeks, so I'll be just fine.  Like the typical Aries that I am, I'll just put my head down and charge right through this.

It is the day before the final chemo and of course I have lots of time for my mind to wander so I start pondering my perceptions of life and death.  I was raised Roman Catholic, so my perception of the world during my younger years was that The Almighty God created Heaven and Earth and that we were bound by his rules (as read to us over and over again during church service or Sunday school), and if we violated them we went to Hell.

Heaven was described as the beautiful happy place where you were never ill, would never want for anything and that everyone you loved, including your pets would be with you.  It was "in the clouds", had no weather other than good and that's about all we heard.  Hell on the other hand, was deep underground, a boiling pit of lava and fire, where those who did not follow Gods rules would go.  I was told, that if I did not come and sit in front of a priest and ask for forgiveness for my sins that I would go to hell and rot in eternity with flames and eternal devils flying all around the place.  Basic damnation.  I have had nightmares my entire life, and I'd say ninety-five percent of them involved the Devil is some shape or form either trying to take me down to hell or trying to take someone I loved down to hell and me fighting to save them.  These were extremely vivid dreams and my active imagination could conjure up all kinds of nasty demons, enough to have me wake up screaming in horror.

This is the basic premise most Christians would

believe, so with this understanding in mind, I have spent a lot of time over the last few months wondering what would happen when I die. I am not a bad person, but I certainly haven't lead the most perfect of lives, so, according to The Christian version of the bible, unless I go to confession, or get absolution from a priest, I am going to spend the rest of my eternity in hell. Which brings me to my mother and my brother. My mother was a kind, loving person, and my brother was more of a believer than I was. Both of them had sad, challenging lives that they did not ask for, but that were brought upon them through the natural course of life. They both worked hard to overcome their challenges and in their own unique ways, especially my bother, connected with their God way before they thought or even knew their time was close. However, according to God's rules, they are now in Hell. There is something very wrong with this picture.

Knowing them as I knew them for over forty years, I knew two people who gave everything of themselves to everyone else for only two reasons, one to help the other person become a better human being and two, to be loved. They both wanted nothing more than to give love and be loved, no matter how awkwardly it may have exhibited itself amongst others, giving was the ultimate driver for both of them. After their deaths I was devastated. However, fortunately I met with a number of my mother's friends who cared for her deeply and took the time to share with me her true measure, one of kindness, gentleness, and sincerity. I am forever grateful to my aunts as well for allowing me to see my mother, as she really was, a beautiful, gentle soul who would do anything for anyone.

I am also thankful that I had an opportunity to meet with close friends of Sean and learn on a more intimate level, the depth of their love for him and the kind of human being he was. The words used, were always, "kind, generous, mentor, loving, always giving, strong, honest, loyal". I heard this over and over again from many people, enough for me to get a really good picture of who he was outside of the man I knew.

So this brings me back to perception and basic beliefs. You see, I believe (yes I admit that I lost my belief for a while), that our lives do not end at our deaths. As I write this I have to double check within myself to ensure I haven't suffered from selective memory loss. You see I was with my mother when she died. Granted, I was snoozing on the floor and was not awake the very moment she took her last breath, but I had been with her for the past two plus weeks, and my sister, who was awake had woken me within minutes if not seconds, so essentially to all intents and purposes, I was there. I was awake; I sat by her side and saw she was gone. I was expecting something magical. I was expecting to feel her spirit in the room. My beloved mother, whom I adored and whom I had begged to come back and communicate with me and who was only a few minutes ago a beautiful living being, was now gone. I waited, for that rush of air, that warm feeling, that possible touch to my heart, the whisper in my ear, it was not there. I held her hand until it became hard and ice cold, I looked into all the corners of the room. Mummy was not there. I did not understand. With Sean I did not have a chance to say goodbye and to ask him to come back, so I understand that he hasn't come back to visit me and say he was okay. On the other hand I had specifically asked mum to come back, to talk to me, to not leave me alone, to let me know how my brother was, but it never happened. It did not happen the day she died, it did not happen within that first week, and no matter how hard I cry and beg and pray, neither one of them have shown themselves to me in my conscious mind to let me know they are okay.

They are okay though. Through the love of a woman I didn't know, who shared a book with me, I have started to learn more about "The other side". Initially my education was just so I could try to understand where my mum and Sean were, and how, if in any way I could communicate with them. Now as I read through the second book, I am reading from the point of view of someone who will be going to the other side sooner than most, and it has afforded me the time to explore what life after death here might look like. Finally for the first time since my mother has died I have met her in dreams, although, there has been a barrier between us, which I am sure will eventually fall away. I have seen that she is not in "heaven" or "hell" as the Catholic Church would lead us to believe. Rather, she is in a place where she is happy. I don't know anything about that place yet, and have yet to meet with my brother, but I believe they are both there, and that when he is ready, or when I am ready, he will show himself to me. This understanding has brought a great sense of healing to my heart. That is not to say I don't feel terrific sadness when I think of them and the huge hole their loss has left in my life that could never be filled, rather it has given me a sense of comfort in knowing that where they are, they are okay. They are happy, and they are watching out for me and for my children.

So without waxing philosophically about all the different ways this could be interpreted, suffice it to say, I'm willing to put a small stick in the sand to say that Yes, I have managed to find some faith again after my heart was cut and smashed to pieces. Yes I believe there is a life beyond what we currently know, although I don't know enough to be able to explain it. No, I'm still not over the loss of my mother and my brother but I am now comfortable in a certain knowledge that they still exist in a different realm and that every single night when I go to sleep I call to them, and let them know I'm on my way to visit them and for them to be ready to see me. So far Sean is deaf to this, but Mummy has shown up once, so I keep on trying.

If there is one thing everyone can say about me it is that I am persistent as hell.

THE FUTURE

Here I am sitting at Lions Gate Hospital waiting for my chemo to start. Today is my first Herceptin only treatment and I'm looking forward to experiencing a chemo treatment without the debilitating side effects that Adriamycin, Cyclophosphamide and Taxol bring on. Weird isn't it, to be looking forward to side effects. I guess that's how dramatically having cancer changes your life. You celebrate the little victories, like a day without pain, or look forward to such things as lesser side effects and the day you can feel the ends of your fingers properly again.

I am so happy to have the yucky chemo behind me, although, believe it or not, my chemo session last week was great fun. Well, the session itself was fun because I had lots of visitors and we shared champagne and celebrated the end of the "bad" chemo. The week after the chemo was not fun as the side effects were really bad (after twelve weeks of build up), and I'm still actually feeling them today. I think the Neupogen shots are responsible for most of the pain and swelling, so I'm relieved I won't have to do those again either.

I got some fantastic news last week. The results of my MRI done on November 13th were revealed to me. They are amazing. Sasha was extremely pleased with my response to chemo, as am I. Could you imagine how devastating it would be to hear the chemo had not worked?  Unfortunately, in my new circle of cancer buddies I have heard of more than one incidence where the chemo has not worked.  The disappointment one must feel having dragged yourself through hell for months to find out that it hasn't been effective would be devastating.

So, as things improve with me, my mind is starting to turn towards the prospect of returning to work.


The idea of returning to work seems so alien to me. Actually it scares me a little.  You see I'm not the person I once was.  I don't feel as confident as I used to.  I feel almost less of a person than I was, so I'm concerned about my ability to do my job effectively.  Until yesterday I was worried that I wouldn't be able to put my heart into it anymore.  Then by pure fluke when I was on the coast yesterday dealing with things related to my mother's estate, I ran into a client of mine.  I couldn't believe it.  He was happy to see me; said things aren't the same without me and asked when I'd be coming back.  It was a great boost to my ego, albeit embarrassing to hear his positive opinion of me and how I had chosen my path and my way of dealing with cancer.  I felt empowered.  I realized everything would be okay.  Actually it will probably be better because I have actually lived and breathed all the reasons why I do what I do.  Being diagnosed with cancer has brought the value of having critical illness insurance right in front of me, has helped me see firsthand why disability insurance is so necessary, and now that I am uninsurable I understand the value of purchasing life insurance when you can because you never know when it will be too late.

I had two visitors to my chemo session today, which is a rare occurrence. The first was from my "big boss" as I call her. It was great to see Joanne and to hear how everything was going at work, as well as to know that I was missed. She also gave me some great advice. You see I'd been told to take mini-break/holiday before my radiation started in January, but I was uncertain about doing so, especially if something were to happen to me while away. Joanne reminded me that I was covered and should take the time to take care for myself and get strong for the onslaught of radiation coming up.........so I think I'll follow her wise words and take off to sunny climes for a little while. I know my body could use the warmth and certainly my psyche could use a little cheering up.

The other visitor I had was my friend Evelyn from the Callanish Retreat. She is a wonderfully sweet girl with such a positive outlook. I really enjoyed getting to know her at the retreat and was thrilled to get a visit today. It made me realize that as human beings, we tend to gravitate to and enjoy the company of people who "get" us. People who have been diagnosed with a serious cancer have been changed in a way that only another cancer patient can understand. It's sort of an unspoken agreement or a connection beyond words where you just know how that person is feeling. It's a shared bond that neither of you signed up for, but now that you're here, being with others of the same ilk brings comfort and a sense of belonging.

When I first got sick, I didn't feel any different than anyone else, but after six months of intense treatment, I do feel different, and I feel like a lesser person. I used to be supremely confident and although I was never beautiful, I always felt attractive and intelligent and worthwhile. Now, I feel extremely unattractive (especially with my hair growing back in like a ninety year old man). I feel mentally diminished and not as "quick" as I used to be, and I also feel like I'm boring to normal people. I don't have normal days anymore, so when going for a glass of wine with a friend, it's hard for me to "chat" about the day. What day? My days are empty. I'm not contributing or doing anything except writing and watching Netflix and cuddling with my dog. Ho hum, that's not interesting to anyone, so what is there to talk about, except perhaps the latest episode of "Lie to Me" or "Dexter".

So the question is, "What can I do to integrate back into society?" That makes me think of prisoners being released after a long time behind bars. Imagine how difficult it must be for them to integrate into society. The world must seem alien and scary to them, as it does a bit for me. That being said, there has to be a way to do it, to slowly come out of my shell and be "normal" again. Aah I see a project for me... find ways to make a come back, like an old rocker! I've got to polish myself back up and figure out a way to get back out to the living.

## GOODBYE 2012

Today is the end of the Mayan Calendar and in some way it was wishful thinking on my part that the world would end today. Okay, perhaps not really wishful thinking, more some sort of sick fantasy. I thought if the entire world ends today then I could see my mother and Sean again, I wouldn't have to go through radiation and surgery and would never have to worry about cancer again. It wasn't that I really wanted everyone else to die; it just seemed to be a "bright side" way of looking at the doom and gloom prophecy.

However, here we all still are, so on I must trudge along this uphill, rocky, slippery and booby trapped path (pun intended) until I can get to the end. What is at the end? I often wonder, what will await me once all this is over. Will it really be over and will I live a long fruitful life until I'm an old codger, or will it return in a year or two and I'll have to start this road all over again. If that happens I'll be royally pissed off!

So, today is day three of radiation therapy. I have to tell you I hate radiation therapy almost more than I hated chemotherapy. It goes against all my knowledge and instinct to voluntarily lie on a bed in an awkward position for forty minutes so I can be blasted by eight to twelve long doses of radiation poisoning. I hate it. Also, I can feel it. I was told it would not hurt until a few weeks in when the skin would begin to blister and crack, but that's a load of baloney.  It hurt from the very first treatment on Wednesday afternoon.  Yesterday I asked the radiologist and he said that yes, for people with light, sensitive Irish type skin like I have, it does hurt, from the beginning.  It feels like a bad sunburn, itchy, burning, stinging, sensitive to the touch, and he said it will only get worse each of the twenty-eight times, not better.  So, he recommended I take painkillers before each session as well as speak to my doctor and the pain management area about meds and dressings to help me when the skin starts to look like bubbly bacon in the frying pan.

My girlfriend Debbie has recommended wine therapy.  It seems much more inviting to me.  Her suggestion is to have a few glasses of wine after each session to dull the pain.  Sounds fantastic, although it also comes with a few not so good things.  Wine everyday will probably cause some other physical damage to my liver, not to mention with my taste in wines, it would be an expensive proposition, so I'll stick to the cheap oral meds the doc will provide.  For posterity purposes, I'm going to try to get a photograph of me all set up in the RADS room, including a photograph of the custom made bolus they use to help my top layer of skin fry more than normal RADS would do - sounds just lovely, just think of it as a thick layer of grease attracting and intensifying the rays to sizzle me a deep dark purple.  Yum, I can smell the burning now.

Christmas for our family is not a celebration.  We all

congregate at dad and Tina's for the usual Christmas Eve dinner, but it is not the same. The atmosphere is tense, everyone is subdued and nobody mentions the elephant in the room, aka, where is Sean. We all do our best to try to celebrate, let the year be gone and thank our lucky stars for the blessings we have, but I cannot help wishing Sean was here and wishing mum was still alive so I could call her in the morning and wish her Merry Christmas. I suppose this, like everything else, is something I need to get used to.

Loss is such a terrible thing and in such a short time my family and I have faced so many losses. For me it has been loss of self, loss of a brother and loss of a mother. I believe that is more than your average dose of pain that one person should endure in a year. Some days I am not sure how I can get up and function in a normal manner, and some days I just stay home and hide.

This year I experienced pain like I never have before. I was defeated, beat down and crushed to a pulp. I was kicked in the ass, picked back up and then kicked back down again. I was told I was going to die, I was shocked by my brother's death and I watched my mother die. I came face to face with my mortality. I wish I could say my battle is now, but unfortunately that part of the story is still to be told. I don't believe any more tragedy can strike me right now, I am sure I have the stamp of immunity upon me, however, I must still deal with the end of radiation and then surgery along with continued chemotherapy in order to rid my body of the disease that attacked me merely a short nine or ten months ago.

I consider 2012 to be the year that I died, the year that changed me forever. There is not a morning that I wake up without thinking of Sean and my mother. There is not a day that goes by without me having the desire to call mum and share something with her, and there is not an evening when I go to sleep that I do not make a silent wish that they were still here or a plea for them to hear me and visit me. The pain has not gone, rather it has found a way to hide, to keep dormant and allow me to live a functional life. However every so often it wells up like a deep-rooted vine and overwhelms me. It suffocates my mind, grabs hold of my heart and pulls me to my knees. It humbles me. It hits me at my core and reminds me of my vulnerability.

I am a human being after all, susceptible to emotions, pain, grief and joy. People say my experiences this year have made me stronger. I disagree, I think they have made me more aware of how fragile our lives are, how we must treasure and live every moment and how we must never, ever take anything for granted. I wish we could all know this without having to go through tragedy, however that seems to be the human drama. What is life without a little tragedy?

Next time around, could the powers that be please hand mine down in a little smaller portion?

Dear Reader;

If you would like to continue to follow my story and read how my cancer treatments are progressing, you can find me on my blog page: www.pammenteryoung.com.

You can also find me on Facebook www.facebook.com/MichellePammenterYoung.    Please like my page.

Thank you for reading my book and please spread the word about Inflammatory Breast Cancer.

With love,
Michelle

Made in the USA
Charleston, SC
29 May 2013